Competency-Based Resumes

How to
Bring Your
Resume to
the Top of
the Pile

By

Robin Kessler

and

Linda A. Strasburg

CAREER
PRESS

Franklin Lakes, NJ

COMPETENCY-BASED RESUMES
EDITED BY KRISTEN PARKES
TYPESET BY EILEEN DOW MUNSON
Cover design by DesignConcept
Printed in the U.S.A. by Book-mart Press

To order this title, please call toll-free 1-800-CAREER-1 (NJ and Canada: 201-848-0310) to order using VISA or MasterCard, or for further information on books from Career Press.

CAREER
PRESS

The Career Press, Inc., 3 Tice Road, PO Box 687,
Franklin Lakes, NJ 07417
www.careerpress.com

Library of Congress Cataloging-in-Publication Data

Kessler, Robin, 1955-
  Competency-based resumes : how to bring your resume to the top of the pile / by Robin
Kessler and Linda A. Strasburg.
    p. cm.
  Includes index.
  ISBN 1-56414-772-X (paper)
    1. Resumes (Employment) I. Strasburg, Linda A., 1948- II. Title.

HF5383.K47 2005
650.14′2--dc22

                                                              2004054483

As we transition from an Industrial age to an Information age/Knowledge worker economy, we need a new mindset, a new skill set, and a new tool set. **Competency-Based Resumes** reflects that transition with a cornucopia of practical, tested, insightful resume ideas and guidelines.

—Dr. Stephen R. Covey, author,
The 7 Habits of Highly Effective People and
The 8th Habit: From Effectiveness to Greatness

Dedication

This is for my mother, Shirley Kessler, who taught me that I could do anything I really wanted; and in memory of my father, Barney Kessler, who helped me learn to think for myself and made it possible for me to get a great education. I hope he would be proud. Their competencies have always helped me identify my own.

—Robin Kessler

This book is dedicated to my mother, Lillyan Loomis, who always believed in my competencies even before I did; my late husband, Jerry R. Bell, who wished for me the best of life and who is still by my side guiding me to be more competent; and my grandchildren, Andre, Xochi, and Giovanni, who will contribute their many competencies to a better future.

—Linda A. Strasburg

Acknowledgments

We have more people to thank for helping with this book than we could ever name. But here are a few who deserve some special recognition.

Thank you to Bill Baumgardt, my ex-manager and friend, for taking the time to review the manuscript one evening during his business trip to Houston. To Hank Radoff, my cousin and friend, for handling our legal work. To Mary Alice Eureste, for encouraging me to learn more about competencies. To David Heath, for confirming the need for competency-based resumes in corporations using competency-based systems. To Nancy Palma and Patty Frederick, our accountant and bookkeeper, for keeping us out of trouble.

To Ron Fry, Mike Lewis, and Mike Pye at Career Press, thank you for understanding our idea and believing in it. To Kristen Parkes, for her skills as an editor and consistent professionalism during the process.

To my family and friends, thank you for your patience during these months I've been working on the book. Even though I value all of you, I want to mention a few special people who have been important to me for a long time. To my aunts and uncles, Florence and Bob Lait, Paul Kessler, Louise Colin, and Rae and Milt Goldberg, for their encouragement. To Pam Thompson, who knew how to be a good friend from the very beginning; and to Paula Hanson, who has had the wisdom to help me feel sane since graduate school, please know how much I value your friendship. To Archie Thompson and Andy Hanson, their husbands, thank you for your friendship and warmth as hosts.

To the teachers who inspired me: Sarah Day Haynes at Longfellow Elementary School, Jean Price at Bellaire High School, and Dr. Carl Smith, Dr. Irwin Weil, and Professor Dennis Brutus at Northwestern University.

Here's to all of you!

—Robin Kessler

Thanks to all of my family, friends, clients, students, and radio listening audiences who asked the difficult questions and who challenged old notions while offering new solutions. Without the questions, there would be no new answers; without challenging old notions, I would have languished; without offering new solutions, I would not have created.

—Linda A. Strasburg

Table of Contents

Chapter 1

Meet the New Competency-Based Strategy

If you ran for political office and won the majority of the popular vote, would you assume you'd won the election? Not if you expected to be the next president of the United States. Understanding that electoral college votes determine who wins the presidency is critical if you plan to run for—and win—that office.

Understanding the number of points you'll need to win a tennis match is key in determining your strategy to beat your opponent.

If the wind changes, you'd better plan to tack and reset your sails, if you want to make it to the right dock.

Understanding how systems work can increase your ability to get what you want. But we need to realize that systems change and grow. We can expect the systems we work with to continue changing, and we can expect the pace of change to only get faster.

When systems change, we need to recognize what is happening as early as possible to help us develop the strategy to allow us to maneuver more effectively and reach our goal. We need to carefully watch for those changes. We have to be smarter than our competitors, anticipate change, and adjust our own approach if we want to be successful now and in the future—and perhaps even to survive!

The system behind finding a good job has changed. Employers have changed the system. If you want to be successful in today's job market, you need every edge over your competition. *You* need to change.

Understanding the system when looking for a job has always given certain candidates the advantage with employers. **But it is critical to realize and accept that the system that employers use when making the decision to fill jobs has changed significantly in the last few years and continues to change today.**

Candidates need to tailor their approach to adjust to the employers' changes—and target their candidacy to emphasize what the employers want.

Imagine getting ready to run a race and finding out that the race had changed from a 5k run to a half marathon. If you wanted to win the race badly enough, you'd change the way you train and develop a new strategy.

This book will give you the new strategy—the tools you need—to play the game more effectively and *compete to win*. If you use this approach, you will improve your chance to:

★ Win your ideal job in a new company.

★ Be selected for extremely competitive positions.

★ Get the promotion or new position within your organization.

★ Increase your salary by ensuring employers know how your competencies can improve their results.

★ Be more challenged and happier with your work.

> **You are what you have learned from the past, what you experience today, and what you dream for tomorrow.**

What's Changed?

Unemployment rates are significantly higher than they were in the late 1990s. Sophisticated employers are increasingly using *competency-based systems* to define jobs, and train, select, and promote employees. And we're seeing more jobs posted on the Internet (and in advertisements) asking candidates about their experience in certain key areas, also known as ***competencies***.

What are competencies? Paul Green, in his book *Building Robust Competencies* (Jossey-Bass, 1999), gives one definition used by many HR professionals: **"An individual competency is a written description of measurable work habits and personal skills used to achieve a work objective."**

When competencies are used at the organization level to help achieve organization objectives or goals, they are typically referred to as *core competencies*. Many organizations develop their core competency list and then include the most relevant ones (with additional details) in the list of competencies being developed for job groups and individual positions.

The use of competencies in organizations has expanded significantly in the last decade. More and more organizations are using competency-based applications such as resume screening software, behavioral interviewing, competency-based training, and competency-based pay systems to help them more effectively manage their hiring, training, compensation, and promotion decisions. Many sophisticated companies screen resumes by using software looking for keywords, which are often based upon competencies defined for the position.

Companies such as American Express, IBM, Coca-Cola, Delta Airlines, Anheuser-Busch, PepsiCo, and BP have been among the leaders in using behavioral interviewing techniques, such as Targeted Selection Interviewing, to provide interviewers with better information, based on actual past experience, from candidates.

Effective behavioral interviewing is based on the theory that past behavior is the best predictor of future behavior. In other words, past success predicts future success.

Interviewers ask questions to assess how *competent* candidates are in several areas (or *competencies*) the employer has identified as critical to performance for that specific job. Organizations, in some cases, are trying to hire candidates to specifically build the competencies needed organization-wide. Many companies have trained interviewers to conduct interviews this way since the 1980s, and more organizations have adopted behavioral interviewing since then—even for interviews to be promoted or transferred to new positions within an organization.

Using behavioral interviewing techniques is now standard practice within most sophisticated organizations. But almost all candidates continue to write resumes and prepare for their interviews the same way they did in the past. They have not adapted to the change in how employers conduct their interviews.

 Hint: If you want to improve your chance of winning positions at these top employers, you *must* take advantage of opportunities to emphasize *your* competencies in the key areas the employer needs during the interview—and on your resume. Your examples must be focused, powerful, and concise.

The U.S. Aviation Administration, Waste Management, and the engineering firm Fluor are just three of the organizations that recently posted jobs on Websites that include a listing of competencies (or dimensions) in the job description. The number of organizations listing their positions with clearly identified competencies increases every time we look at employment Websites.

On October 20, 2003, Monster.com (*www.Monster.com*) ran more than 2,000 advertisements asking for competencies. The ads asking for specific competencies came from organizations of all sizes that day and included:

- Sears.
- General Mills.
- HCA.
- Novartis.
- Cummins.
- MetLife.
- Ingersoll-Rand.
- Siemens.
- Dole Food Company.
- Federal Reserve System.
- BP.
- UMass Medical School.
- Abbott Laboratories Employees Credit Union.
- Perot Systems.

Other companies take a more subtle approach. They may include a list of things they are looking for from the ideal candidate in their postings and advertisements—without calling them competencies. If you analyze the more subtle postings, you can identify hidden competencies—and core competency groups—and make the decision to use this information to make your own job search more productive.

 Hint: Take a few minutes and visit some of the Websites of your favorite organizations. Determine if they are using competencies. Type in your profession (for example, "Human Resources") and "Competencies" in your favorite employment Website and see what you find. Notice that competency applications are becoming more and more prevalent in the workplace.

In this book, we will show you how to recognize the clues hidden in these advertisements that others miss. By analyzing the words the employer is using, you can determine what the employer's real needs are. Then we will demonstrate how you can use these clues to write more effective resumes and cover letters that dramatically increase your probability of getting noticed and chosen for an interview.

Using competencies to measure employees and applicants is growing in importance in corporate America and in other sectors including government. The game has changed. And this makes it more important than ever to approach the job search in a new way so that you can compete to win.

Remember, the competition is tougher than ever to get the ideal job.

How Can You Make These Changes Work for You?

How do these changes affect people looking for a job? We believe that candidates must recognize the "system" has changed—and change their own approach to meet the needs of today's employers. In other words, take responsibility for managing your job search in a new way. This will work much more effectively and will give you an edge over the competition.

Candidates need to take the time to position themselves differently than they have in the past to compete and win with employers today.

> It is clear the competition is tough right now. In April 2004, the U.S. unemployment rate was 5.6 percent, and 8.2 million people were classified as unemployed. Check *www.bls.gov* for the most recent U.S. statistics.

Let's imagine you agreed to run a marathon in Colorado. If you live in a part of the country without hills, you'd run on an elevated treadmill or train by running stairs. And you'd make sure to get to the mountains a few days early to give yourself a chance to acclimate.

The demand for people in professions also changes through time. One friend, who worked as a vice president at a tie manufacturing company, lost his job after the trend toward a more casual workplace in the late 1980s and 1990s reduced the demand for ties. Due to changing trends in professions, very few elevator operators or typists are left.

The demand for different skills and different professions keeps changing. In the last five years, information technology went from a hot field during the dot-com boom to significantly less demand in today's market. What can you, as an individual, do? How can you be savvy enough to avoid getting hurt by changes in the economy and the job market?

It's up to you to be smarter and more aware than the competition. You need to be very attentive to changes affecting your profession. We all do.

How This System Will Give You the Tools You Need to Succeed

This book is going to show you how to target employers using competency-based systems—the same employers that are almost always leaders in their industries. This approach will also help you stand out as a candidate with employers who haven't adopted the new systems yet because it is focused on identifying and satisfying the employer's real needs.

How can you compete today to increase your chance of winning an interview for your ideal job and growing professionally? You need to:

1. Understand competency-based systems.

2. Define the competencies employers are looking for in your profession.

3. Create a well-written competency-based resume.

4. Prepare to write competency-based cover letters.

5. Learn to network the competency-based way.

6. Expect and prepare for competency-based interviews.

7. Identify how to actively manage your career in a competency-based system. Know what competencies you need to strengthen to be more successful and where you have competency gaps.

The first key step is to understand competency-based systems. Then you will need to identify the competencies that managers look for in your own professional area.

One of the most productive steps in this process is to write a good quality, competency-based resume. In job search classes, instructors agree that the main purpose of the resume is to help you get interviews. A competency-based resume will give you a significant edge over competitors because the main focus is on highlighting those parts of your background that provide evidence to employers that you have the competencies they are looking for. Your accomplishments should help demonstrate how well developed you are in different competency areas.

Once your resume is ready, you need to think about promoting your competencies and identifying your personal brand. Key ways to do this include strategically writing effective competency-based cover letters, networking and developing your interview skills so that you can answer behavioral questions, based on competencies, effectively. In this book, we will also cover developing materials for your job search using competency-based language and preparing for behavioral or targeted selection interviews.

This is a different, fresh approach. And it is clear that getting hired at many of the most selective employers requires candidates to compete effectively by showing employers their best side—what employers want to see. This is particularly critical in today's job market—when employers usually have the edge.

Creating a competency-based resume will work better for you with almost all employers but will be particularly effective with employers that have made the commitment to strengthen their workforces by:

⋆ Defining competencies.

⋆ Using competencies to advertise for candidates.

⋆ Training managers to use behavioral interviewing techniques when choosing employees.

It is up to you. We're certain that conducting your job search with a competency-based resume and working to improve your skills in handling behavioral, competency-based interviews will give you a significant lead over the competition. Once you get the job, it is also important to realize that understanding how to strengthen and promote your competencies can make a significant difference in how you are valued in the organization. You need to recognize where you have competency strengths and gaps that need to be overcome.

Assuming you've mastered the basics of a job search, using the tools we are going to cover in this book will increase the probability that the hiring manager will recognize that you are a match for the job and give you a strong offer.

Are you ready to approach the job search in a new, more focused way? Let's start now.

> At the end of each chapter we have included a quick question and answer summary for your review. These summaries list the most important points you should understand. Make a point to grasp the concepts and ideas listed before moving to the next chapter.

Key Points for Chapter 1

"An *individual competency* is a written description of measurable work habits and personal skills used to achieve a work objective."

Key Questions	Answers
How can I increase my ability to get the position I want?	Competency-based organizations rely on a different system for looking at what it takes to be successful in jobs, particularly when selecting, promoting, and training their employees. Understanding how competency-based systems work is vital to your success. Surprise: The most important thing to remember is that these systems always change. You need to tailor your approach to adjust to the employer's changes.
What are core competencies?	Core competencies are used at the organization level to help achieve organization objectives or goals.
What are behavioral interview questions?	Interviewers ask questions to assess how **competent** candidates are in several areas. Behavioral interviewing is based on the theory that past behavior is the best predictor of future behavior. In other words, *past success predicts future success.*
What can I do to excel in the competitive job search environment?	To move your resume to the top of the applicant pile and land an interview in this competitive environment, your resume **must be focused (***focused on the competencies desired***), powerful (***use the most potent and powerful action words to describe your competency***), and concise (***make a point, make it clear, use precision wording***).**
Why should I write a competency-based resume?	A competency-based resume will give you a significant edge over competitors because the main focus is on highlighting those parts of your background that *provide evidence* to employers that *you have the competencies* the employer is looking for.
How can I keep promoting my competencies?	It is important to keep marketing your competencies. Other strategic marketing tools are: effective cover letters, networking, and polished interview skills. Remember to focus on the competencies required by the prospective employer.
How are companies using competencies to strengthen their workforce?	They are using competencies to: • Advertise for candidates. • Screen candidate resumes. • Interview using behavioral techniques. • Select employees. • Evaluate employees. • Train employees. • Promote employees. • Reward employees. • Determine assignments. • Decide who should not work for the organization.

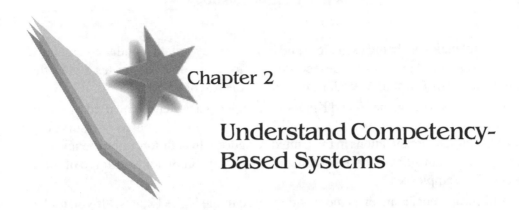

Chapter 2

Understand Competency-Based Systems

Why is it so critical in today's business environment to understand competency-based systems—at least on a basic level? Because competency-based systems are being used more and more by the best organizations to help manage employees. According to Kenneth Carlton Cooper, author of *Effective Competency Modeling and Reporting: A Step-by-Step Guide for Improving Individual & Organizational Performance* (Amacom, 2000), "Competence is one of the hot topics in the world of human resources."

Even though competencies may be a "hot topic" in recent years, the term "competence" has been used this way since at least 1973, when David C. McClelland wrote a paper titled "Testing for Competence Rather than Intelligence." In many colleges, universities, and professional schools, professors have identified competencies their students must become proficient with—and have designed curriculum to teach these competencies to their students for at least 20 years.

Richard Boyatzis is usually credited with coining the term "competencies" in the business environment in his book, *The Competent Manager: A Model for Effective Performance* (John Wiley & Sons), published in 1982. In his book, Boyatzis discussed the results of the large-scale study he conducted looking at which characteristics of managers enabled them to be effective in their jobs. He advocated considering these characteristics—competencies—when selecting, developing, and promoting managers.

In the years since his book was published, organizations from Anheuser-Busch to Carlson Companies, Inc., to more progressive government agencies have identified competencies for their organizations and developed sophisticated systems and processes to recruit, hire, train, appraise, promote, and pay employees based on competencies.

The use of competencies to manage human resources functions continues to grow. According to Signe Spencer, coauthor of *Competence at Work* (John Wiley & Sons, 1993) and a senior consultant at the Hay Group, "In the last 10 years, we have seen an explosion of interest in competency work at all levels worldwide."[1]

Competencies are being used more and more as a key way to identify and manage human resources at many of the best companies to work for in the Unites States, the United Kingdom, Canada, Australia, and most of the rest of the world.

In a recent survey in the United Kingdom, competencies were being used by one in four organizations to recruit or select candidates. This statistic is based on a survey of 747 of the largest organizations in the United Kingdom. In addition, competencies are used by more than 700 UK-based organizations with a combined workforce of more than 4 million employees.[2]

And competencies are even more widely used in the United States. "If you took a broad definition of competencies, my best guess is that about half of the Fortune 500 companies are doing some work with competencies or competency applications," said Ms. Spencer.

Levels of Competency Development

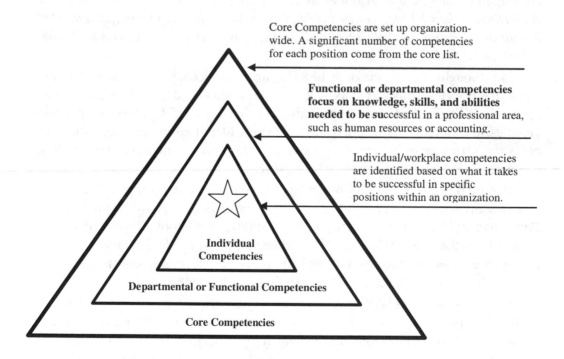

Core Competencies are set up organization-wide. A significant number of competencies for each position come from the core list.

Functional or departmental competencies focus on knowledge, skills, and abilities needed to be successful in a professional area, such as human resources or accounting.

Individual/workplace competencies are identified based on what it takes to be successful in specific positions within an organization.

Individual Competencies

Departmental or Functional Competencies

Core Competencies

What Are Competencies?

In Chapter 1, we provided the definition for competencies Paul Green used in his book: **"An individual competency is a written description of measurable work habits and personal skills used to achieve a work objective."**

Key Elements:

- *Written description*: What are the most accurate words that clearly describe the competency?

- *Measurable work*: What do they mean by measurable? It is the success rate of the work (for example, "Increased sales by 30 percent within one year"). Measurable work includes something quantifiable: an amount, percentage, or time involved to complete the work.

- *Habits and skills*: What are the key habits and skills? Make sure the same word used as a competency is also used in the written description of your skill and habit.

- *To achieve a work objective*: What was accomplished? The outcome or effect of your work is important. Ask how your work saved time or money, or improved the process. How did it benefit the organization?

Another definition of an individual competency says that it:

- ⋆ Is a cluster of related knowledge, attitudes, and skills that affects a major part of one's job.
- ⋆ Correlates with performance on the job.
- ⋆ Can be measured against well-accepted standards.
- ⋆ Can be improved via training and development.[3]

In *Competence at Work*, Lyle and Signe Spencer define a competency as "an underlying characteristic of an individual that is causally related to criterion-referenced effective or superior performance in a job or situation."[4] To explain competencies another way, when Signe Spencer was asked to come up with a less complicated definition, she said that a competency is something about you that helps you do a better job.

Some organizations use this definition for competencies: underlying characteristics, behavior, knowledge, and skills required to differentiate performance. They define what superior performers do more often, in more situations, and with better results.

FedEx Ground developed a presentation about its use of competencies for the 2002 American Society of Training & Development (ASTD) conference. In the presentation, the company says that "competency identification and development are core to leveraging our resources to increase the effectiveness of our employees over the long term. Competencies provide a...

★ Common language for skill identification and people development.

★ Focus for development and performance discussions.

★ Set of key behaviors employees use to increase their effectiveness.

★ A human side to accountability; the knowledge, skills, and abilities that the employee brings to the job."

Although the definition can be more complex, it is also important to think about competencies as the knowledge, skills, and abilities needed to be effective in a job. There are basically three main levels at which competencies can be developed: organization-wide, departmental or functional, and at the individual job level.

Core competencies may be identified for the organization as a whole. Departmental or functional competencies are identified to encourage more specific knowledge, skills, and abilities that people in a particular department must have—or in a function-wide area, such as human resources or finance. Individual competencies, sometimes called workplace competencies, are developed based upon the knowledge, skills, and abilities needed to be successful in different positions within the organization. Some organizations develop just core competencies for their organization; some identify and work with all three competency tiers.

In many organizations, competencies are defined based upon different levels of positions. For example, the following table looks at the competency "Planning and Organizing."[5]

Planning and Organizing: The ability to visualize a sequence of actions needed to achieve a goal and to estimate the resources required. A preference for acting in a structured, thorough manner.

Level 1. Professional or Supervisor (U.S.), Junior Manager (UK)

- Manages own time and personal activities.
- Breaks complex activities into manageable tasks.
- Identifies possible obstacles to planned achievement.

Level 2. Middle Manager

- Produces contingency plans for possible future occurrences.
- Estimates in advance the resources and time scales needed to meet objectives.
- Coordinates team activities to make the best use of individual skills and specialties.

Level 3. Senior Manager

- Identifies longer term operational implications of business plans.
- Effectively plans utilization of all resources.

Because the purpose of this book is to help you develop an effective competency-based resume, we are going to encourage you to think about the highest level work that you've done in each competency area—and to be less concerned about any levels the organization has defined, unless they are relevant to your situation.

What Are Competency-Based Systems?

Some organizations identify competencies because they are interested in using them for one particular application—such as developing more targeted, competency-based training. Other organizations have developed a more complete approach and use competencies systematically to help them manage their employees in almost every human resources area.

In most cases, organization leaders become interested in defining competencies and using competency-based applications because they see it as the best way to:

⭐ Build their organization's capability.

⭐ Improve the organization's ability to reach goals.

If you want to work for an organization that uses competencies to determine who gets an interview, which candidates are offered positions, who gets what training, who is promoted, and who gets the best salary increases, you need to understand how the system works and be savvy enough to make sure the decision-makers know how strong you are—in the competencies they care the most about.

We have discussed the basic applications currently being used in competency-based systems including recruitment and selection, training, performance evaluations, and pay. Once competencies are defined, companies and departments can make the decision to use one or more of the applications, such as competency-based training or selection. Most of the more sophisticated companies use almost all of the applications.

In a competency-based system, many of the organizations work with specialized software to screen resumes and choose who will get the interview. When the human resources professional or manager works with the software, they are asked to identify *keywords* that a strong candidate for the position is most likely going to have on his or her resume. The keywords often include competencies, synonyms of competencies, or phrases someone with a particular competency is likely to use. If you submit a resume that does not include a high percentage of these words, the screening software will not select it, the human resources professional will not review it, and you will not get an interview.

During the interview process, companies train their interviewers to use behavioral interviewing questions developed to assess the candidate on key characteristics—competencies—for the position that they are interviewing to fill. For example, a sales manager would probably have "Customer Orientation" as one of his competencies, and would be asked behavioral questions to assess how strong he was in that area. Some organizations even structure their interview process so that their interviewers are given a choice of a few questions that are already developed for each competency area.

Performance reviews are often based on how *competent* employees are perceived to be on a list of competencies that are sometimes called dimensions or characteristics. Employers take the results of the appraisals and use them, in addition to some discussion with the managers, to determine training needs based upon where the employee is weak in some critical competencies or needs. This is also known as competency-based training, and the "missing" or weak competencies are also known as competency gaps. Decisions about salary increases, ranking of employees, and even who will leave the organization are often based on the results of how competent employees are perceived to be.

What's Missing From the Current Competency-Based Systems?

Even the most advanced companies, who are going out of their way to develop wonderful and effective competency-based systems, are not developing their internal resumes so that key managers clearly know all the accomplishments of their employees in each competency area.

 Hint: Don't settle for envisioning how things should be; visualize how things can and will be.

What resources do managers not know about because they have not asked or the employee does not communicate or promote himself well? How many organizations have a change in management, and the new manager has to learn who is the best person to give assignments to—before they really know the competencies of their new employees?

When good competency-based systems are already in place, developing better, more effective competency-based resumes is the next step toward strategically managing and developing an even more progressive human resources partnership with employees.

How many internal resumes are well-written and emphasize the competencies the organization cares about? Wouldn't a competency-based resume help managers know their employees' knowledge, skills, and abilities better and increase their ability to utilize their employees' strengths more strategically? How many employees feel they are underutilized because their management doesn't know that they are competent in areas other than the ones they are currently demonstrating?

The best competency systems help managers at all levels know the resources they have in their departments. What percentage of senior level managers managing large groups of people realize they have resources in their department that they may not know about? If an employee lived in China before college and spoke Mandarin and Cantonese, how would the senior manager know that he had the language skills and understood the culture? The senior manager would if he worked in an organization with a well-designed, complete competency-based system.

If an employee is bilingual and wrote or translated a technical manual in Spanish five years ago at his last employer, senior level managers need to be aware of this valuable resource in their department. Often they aren't.

And if a human resources professional worked on a college or high school newspaper staff, would her manager realize she just might be able to write manuals, articles, or even a book? Only if their organization had developed a competency-based system with information that the employees had a chance to contribute to.

Can you see why this concept is growing?

We believe competency-based resumes give managers the ability to better recognize the talents of current employees—and certainly to identify the competencies of potential employees. Competency-based resumes need to be part of any sophisticated competency-based system in organizations.

The new model, which includes competency-based resumes and some training or coaching for employees on how to promote their own careers in a competency-based system, makes competency-based systems more complete and gives employees an opportunity to ensure their managers are more aware of their own competencies.

Key Points for Chapter 2	
"In the last 10 years, we have seen an explosion of interest in competency work at all levels worldwide." —Signe Spencer, coauthor of *Competencies at Work*	
Key Questions	**Answers**
What are some definitions of competencies?	Competencies are: • Underlying characteristics, behavior, knowledge, and skills required to differentiate performance. • Characteristics that define what superior performers do more often, in more situations, and with better results. • Something about you that helps you do a better job. • A written description of measurable work habits and personal skills used to achieve a work objective. • A collection of related knowledge, attitudes, and skills that affects a major part of one's job. • Linked with performance on the job. • Measured against well-accepted standards. • Improved with training and development.
Why have so many organizations adopted competency-based systems?	Competencies provide a: • Common language for skill identification and people development. • Focus for development and performance discussions. • Set of key behaviors employees use to increase their effectiveness. • Human side to accountability; the knowledge, skills, and abilities that the employee brings to the job."

Key Points for Chapter 2 (continued)	
Key Questions	**Answers**
At what levels within an organization are competencies developed?	There are three main levels at which competencies are developed: organization-wide, departmental or functional, and at the individual job level. • Core competencies may be identified for the organization as a whole. • Departmental or functional competencies are identified to encourage more specific knowledge, skills, and abilities in a department or functional area. • Individual competencies are developed based upon the knowledge, skills, and abilities needed to be successful in different positions within the organization. In many organizations, competencies are defined based upon different levels such as professional, supervisor, middle manager, and senior manager.
Which level do I target? I have competencies at many different levels.	Look at the levels identified by the organization for the position you are interested in. Then, think about the highest level work that you've done in each competency area and include those in your resume.
Are there any other terms used for competencies?	Competencies are sometimes called dimensions, characteristics, or keys to success. They may also be listed as values.
How are competencies used for training and employee development?	Performance reviews are often based on how *competent* employees are perceived to be on a list of competencies. Employers take the completed appraisals and use them to determine training needs. Some organizations ask their employees to identify competency gaps and then schedule training courses.
The best competency systems help managers at all levels know the resources they have in their departments.	
How can I use my new competency-based resume to advance within my organization?	Here's what you can do: • Identify the target position within your organization. • List competencies for that position by interviewing the managers of that department, talking to people who have held that position, and reading organizational competency listings. • Identify competency gaps and find ways to fill the gaps with training, volunteering, and education. • Keep track of your accomplishments and how they relate to the desired competencies. • Update your resume periodically. • Market your competencies to the right people.

Chapter 3

Identify Relevant Competencies

"Would you tell me, please, which way I ought to go from here?"
"That depends a good deal on where you want to get to," said the Cat.
"I don't much care where—" said Alice.
"Then it doesn't matter which way you go," said the Cat.
"As long as I get somewhere," Alice added as an explanation.
"Oh, you're sure to do that," said the Cat, "if you only walk long enough."

—Lewis Carroll, *Alice's Adventures in Wonderland*

Unlike the Cheshire-Cat, we think you need to know as much as possible about where you're going before you start your journey. Before we begin to write any resumes, we need to figure out what the hiring manager and the organization are looking for. Competencies are the right place to start.

**Even if you are on the right track,
you'll get run over if you just sit there.**

Some organizations have already identified competencies for their positions and routinely listed them in advertisements and job descriptions. Other companies have not used the word "competencies" (or similar words such as "dimensions," "values," or "behavioral expressions") but, in reality, they are actually looking for competencies in their job requirements or other parts of their advertisements.

By having this list—or figuring out what are likely to be identified as competencies for the job you want, you can develop a resume targeted to the employer's needs. Writing a competency-based resume will give you an edge with these employers.

When Organizations Have Identified Competencies

If the competencies have been identified for the position, they may be listed under a heading called "Competencies" or "Dimensions" in the job posting or advertisement.

More and more of the organizations posting jobs online are directly listing relevant competencies in their ads. When the competencies are not directly identified, you need to do several things to begin to identify the competencies for the position on your own. The four major steps to identify the competencies are:

1. Think about what the obvious competencies would be for the position.

2. Look at advertisements and postings from competitors.

3. Compile a list of competencies from other sources, including employment Websites, advertisements in newspapers and magazines, professional associations, and the organization's Website.

4. Select 10 to 15 competencies that would be the *most* critical for the position you are interested in from Appendices A and B.

For example, Bank of America listed an opportunity on Monster.com in February 2004 for a Senior Process Design Engineer in Richmond, Virginia. In the advertisement "Critical Competencies" were listed as:

★ Extensive Project Management knowledge and experience.

★ Strong verbal and written communication.

★ Negotiation and facilitation skills.

★ Strong leadership and organizational skills, with attention to detail.

★ Strong skills in MS Office, MS Project, Visio.

When you already work for an organization, you may be able to find the relevant list of competencies for individual jobs or job levels:

★ On the company's Website.

★ On performance reviews for employees currently in the position.

★ Listed in different company handbooks or manuals.

★ By asking a friend who works in the relevant department in the organization.

We *are* encouraging you to be resourceful and make every effort to find this list—if the organization has taken the time to develop it.

If the competencies aren't directly identified, look further.

The First Step

Think about what the obvious competencies would be for the position.

Read the posting or advertisement to see if the competencies are listed under a heading such as "Requirements." If you look at the positions that are listed at American Express's Website, you will not see the word "competencies," but you will see phrases and words that look a lot like obvious core and individual competencies under the heading "Required Qualifications."

The Second Step

Look at advertisements and postings from competitors for equivalent positions to see if they have directly listed the competencies they've identified for the position. Then try to determine if the same competencies work for the position you are interested in, or if they need to be reworked and modified.

The Third Step

Begin to compile a comprehensive list of competencies for your position.

There are a number of places you can go to get a broader list of competencies for a particular position. For example, if you are interested in being considered for a human resources manager's position at a company that has not listed competencies in its advertisement, go to:

⭐ An employment Website such as Monster.com or CareerBuilder.com, and type in "competencies human resources manager." Look at several ads and determine if the competencies that are identified for those positions match what you know about the position you are interested in.

⭐ The Websites for companies that are competitors to the organization that has the position you want. Look for human resources manager positions that are posted in the careers/jobs/employment section of their Website.

⭐ Employment advertisements in newspapers, association publications, and other sources to see if any of their ads for similar positions have listed competencies.

⭐ Your professional association Website (for human resources, you would want to go to *www.shrm.org* or to the associations for professional areas within human resources—for training and development, try *www.astd.org* and for compensation, try *www.worldatwork.org*). Look at job opportunities listed to see if the organization has identified competencies for the position. Also consider using the research capabilities of the association, which may be online or through a research professional who works for the organization, to help you identify typical competencies.

⭐ The Website from the organization you are interested in. Can you find information giving you clues about the corporate culture? One place to glean some information is the organization's mission, vision, or values (which may be online). Read the company's annual report—particularly the letters from the chairman and CEO. See if you can sense what its values are—or where the organization is feeling pain or having problems. Both can give you some clues as to the competencies the organization needs to be successful in the future.

> **Key Element:** Notice the approach we are presenting here is very different from writing resumes in the past. The competency-based resume approach always looks at what the employer needs first. Then write your resume based on *the employer's* needs. The traditional way to write resumes is to look at *your* background first by focusing on your skills and accomplishments and then hope to match them to a job opening.
>
> **A compelling competency-based resume *always* considers the needs of the employer first.**

Ask yourself what competencies you would look for if you were the hiring manager. Analyze the advertisement or job posting and look for words, or synonyms for those words, that might be on a competency listing.

Identify what you think the most relevant competencies would be from a list of core competencies and individual competencies targeted to your own professional area. Most organizations typically identify between eight and 12 competencies.[1] Then think about the level of expertise within that competency area that the organization would probably need for the position you are interested in.

Here's a list of the most standard competencies used by organizations:[2]

1. Achievement/Results Orientation.
2. Initiative.
3. Impact and Influence.
4. Customer Service Orientation.
5. Interpersonal Understanding.
6. Organizational Awareness.
7. Analytical Thinking.
8. Conceptual Thinking.
9. Information Seeking.
10. Integrity.

Interestingly, the list of the 10 most common competencies in the United Kingdom is a little different.[3]

1. Team Orientation.
2. Communication.
3. People Management.
4. Customer Focus.
5. Results-Orientation.

6. Problem-Solving.

7. Planning and Organizing.

8. Technical Skills.

9. Leadership.

10. Business Awareness and Decision-Making (tied).

In addition to seeing that even countries sharing the same language can have different priorities for competencies, within each country you can have organizations with different needs—and different competencies.

Each organization develops its own list of competencies, and the list can be dramatically different based upon the culture and goals of the organization. Organizations that pride themselves on being progressive, such as Celestial Seasonings and Ben and Jerry's, would probably emphasize different competencies than a more conservative corporation would to be consistent with the corporate culture it is trying to create.

Depending on its business purpose or strategy, the organization may prioritize different competencies. For example, if the corporation's strategy is to be the lowest-cost producer or if the organization's vision depends on innovation, the competencies defined and emphasized may be very different. When an organization's needs change, the competencies needed may also change. Despite these considerations, it is reasonable to expect that most of the list of 10 standard competencies would be on many organizations' lists.

The lists of competencies included throughout this book and in the appendices are almost always ranked in order by the relative frequency with which each competency distinguishes superior from average performers. The exception is the first list of "Most Standard Competencies" in this chapter, which are simply the 10 most common competencies (not in a specific order).

According to Signe Spencer, the biggest change to the list in the last few years is the growing importance of the competency "integrity." Integrity is seen as particularly important at the higher levels of organizations.[4]

Because each organization may identify different important competencies, and functions within organizations may have different needs, we've provided a more complete list of competencies in Appendices A and B to look through.

The list of competencies included in Appendix A was identified by the authors Edward J. Cripe and Richard S. Mansfield in their book *The Value-Added Employee* (Butterworth-Heinemann, 2002). The focus is on 31 major competencies, along with some behaviors associated with each.

The Fourth Step

Look through the list of competencies included in Appendices A and B carefully. Check off the competencies that are the most significant for the position you are interested in. Then go back and edit your list based upon which competencies you think the hiring manager would identify. Limit the list to the 10 to 15 most important.

So now you've selected the competencies that would be the *most* critical for the position you are interested in being considered for. Identify if there are some functional or individual position competencies that you think the hiring organization would put on the list. For example, as an engineer, you would expect the competencies to include much more emphasis on specific competencies such as technical knowledge in subsea engineering or rotating equipment.

Because the typical organization identifies eight to 12 competencies, we suggest that your list should ideally include 10 to 20 competencies to improve the chance that your list includes those competencies that the organization selected. Consider how important each competency is to being successful in the position. Many organizations using competency-based selection methods either rank or put weightings on each competency based on the level of the position in the organization or their perception of the overall importance of the competency to success in the job.

Depending on the level of the position, the organization would need different levels of knowledge, skills, and ability within each competency. For example, to be successful, a senior-level human resources professional or manager would need more organizational awareness and be expected to work more independently than a junior-level human resources professional with a recent degree. An organization would expect organizational awareness and initiative from both levels, but would require a higher level of competency from the senior human resources professional.

While recognizing that organizations may define different levels of expertise for each competency based upon experience and other factors, we believe that the focus for writing an effective competency-based resume should be on identifying the most critical competencies and your *strongest* accomplishments in each competency area— not focusing on the different levels of competency achievement.

So at this point, you have a list of competencies to use when writing your resume. Check the list against competitors. Keep looking for competencies included in online and newspaper ads. Ask your best networking contacts and mentors if they agree with the list you've put together. Accept that you may change the list as you receive new information.

Congratulations—you've completed the first major step. Now we are ready to begin working on your resume.

Key Points for Chapter 3	
"In order to aim the arrow, you must see the target."	
Key Questions	**Answers**
What is the first step toward identifying the *right* competencies to use in a competency-based resume?	Look first at the advertisement, posting, or job description from the organization. We are seeing more organizations than ever before being direct and listing the competencies they need.
If the organization *didn't* provide a list of the competencies they are looking for: How do I get started compiling my list of key competencies? Where do I find some clues as to what these competencies should be?	• Think about what competencies would be obvious for the position. • Look at advertisements and postings from competitors for equivalent positions to see if they have directly listed the competencies they've identified for the position. Then try to determine if the same competencies work for the position you are interested in. • Visit an employment Website such as Monster or CareerBuilder.com and look at equivalent jobs for competency lists. • Look at the Websites for companies that are competitors to the organization that has the position you want. • Find employment advertisements in newspapers, association publications, and other sources and see if you can glean typical competencies for the professional area. • Read through your professional association Website thoroughly, and use their research support to identify competencies • Go to the Website from the organization you are interested in and read through its publications to find information giving you clues about its culture and values.
What are some of the most typical competencies used by organizations?	Here's a list of the most standard competencies used by organizations: 　1.　Achievement/Results Orientation. 　2.　Initiative. 　3.　Impact and Influence. 　4.　Customer Service Orientation. 　5.　Interpersonal Understanding. 　6.　Organizational Awareness. 　7.　Analytical Thinking. 　8.　Conceptual Thinking. 　9.　Information Seeking. 　10.　Integrity. *Remember these are the most standard and are by no means the only competencies that may be desired by your target organization.* Each organization develops its own list of competencies, and the list can be dramatically different based upon the culture and goals of the organization.

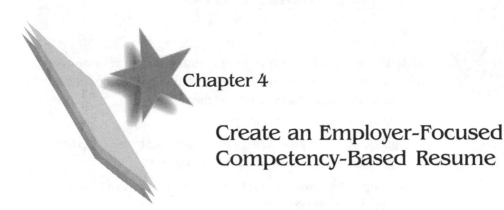

Chapter 4

Create an Employer-Focused Competency-Based Resume

Why Should You Develop a Competency-Based Resume?

The first major reason: Competency-based resumes are much better than most conventional resumes at emphasizing how your knowledge, experience, and skills match the position.

It's almost like wearing the right shade of your school color when you return for homecoming. Other alumni will be able to immediately recognize that you belong to their group—that you *fit* what they expect to see one of their alums to look like.

In essence, we are going to teach you to point out competencies the decision-maker is looking for so the *fit* is obvious. Competency-based resumes make it easier for people making the hiring decisions to see what skills you have and what you have done to demonstrate you can do the job, exceed business goals, increase profit, and save time or money.

Career consultants generally agree that the major purpose of the resume is to help candidates get an interview. Having a competency-based resume will help convince hiring managers, human resources, and recruiters that you have the skills and competencies they are looking for—that you are worth interviewing—and eventually worth hiring.

The second major reason: Competency-based resumes focus on the employer's needs. Competency-based resumes work more effectively because the emphasis is on the organization's needs first.

Traditionally, when career consultants work with candidates to develop their resumes, they help individuals identify their strengths and accomplishments and explain them in a clear way when writing the actual resume. The emphasis is on the individual's background—not the employer's needs.

In contrast, competency-based resumes work well because they put the emphasis on what the employer needs. When you write a competency-based resume, it will be very clear that you fit what they are looking for.

Hint: The approach to writing competency-based resumes is different from the way you have written traditional resumes in the past. We recommend that you follow these steps:

1. Identify competencies for the position.

2. Think about what you have done that demonstrates expertise or experience with each of the competencies.

3. Develop accomplishment statements for as many of the competencies as you can.

4. Write the summary section so it emphasizes your experience and strengths related to the key competencies for the position. Include relevant information and personalize the section if there's enough space.

5. Determine which competency-based resume format— chronological, functional, direct competency, or combination—best fits your needs, and prepare your first draft of the resume.

6. Remember to include sections on your education and any other specific information relevant to potential employers.

7. Add additional competency-related accomplishment statements, and if you still have space, other accomplishment statements.

8. Prioritize competency-related phrases in your summary section and competency-based accomplishments within the appropriate sections of the resume.

9. Review and polish your resume. Ask other professionals for input.

10. Finalize your resume. Develop an electronic version of the resume with a keyword summary section.

Who Can Benefit From Using a Competency-Based Resume?

We are confident you will present yourself more effectively to decision-makers and hiring managers if you use a competency-based resume.

Here's a list of the benefits of developing a competency-based resume and using it to market yourself. Competency-based resumes will:

★ Confirm to the employer that you have the expertise, or competency, they are looking for.

★ Improve your chance of being selected for interviews for the positions that you want.

⭑ Help you be perceived as more clearly competitive.

⭑ Enable you to explain sticky areas in your background in a more positive way.

One recent client had been looking for a job for more than 20 months when we began working with him to develop his resume and coach him on searching for a new position. He was, by that time, in some financial trouble, and his confidence was shaken.

We helped him develop a competency-based resume to emphasize the competencies that the best employers would be looking for when they wanted to hire a sales professional. We also worked with him until he could clearly explain his own background in computer peripheral sales, his strengths, and what he wanted in his next position.

During our first session, it became obvious that he had some significant sales results and awards but had not clearly shown them on his resume or talked about them effectively during his interviews.

Within five weeks of finishing the competency-based resume, he had accepted a new position as a district sales manager at a major telecommunications company, and turned down two other good opportunities.

Competency-based resumes will work equally well for you. They will give you the edge over your true competitors with similar backgrounds.

What Does a Competency-Based Resume Look Like?

At first glance, competency-based resumes look just like other resumes. The change is subtle but powerful.

Here's an example of how a targeted, competency-based resume was developed for an IT manager at American Express interested in being considered for a promotion within his company. We'll go through the steps used to create his competency-based resume.

> A detailed resume summary checklist is provided in Chapter 9, which includes all of the following steps.

1. **Identify competencies for the position.**

In this case, the manager knew that his company had defined competencies for most managerial positions and that they routinely used behavioral questions based on those competencies during the interview. He recognized the benefits of developing a competency-based resume immediately and knew that it would help him get the interview within his company.

CORPORATE SERVICES
EXPENSE MANAGEMENT SOLUTIONS

Overview of Leadership Competencies

The leadership competencies are the foundation for the development plan:

Develops Winning Strategies

Takes a broad perspective and clearly links strategies to plans and objectives. Demonstrates a strong knowledge of external competitor activity and market trends. Understands the key business drivers; uses financial and other business or commercial information to identifies business opportunities.

Drives Results

Takes personal accountability for achieving individual and shared goals. Sets robust plans well in advance and initiates action to move projects forward. Aims for stretch targets. Adjusts actions to respond and capitalize on changing circumstances. Manages time effectively, monitoring performance against deadlines and milestones.

Focuses on the Customer & Client

Proactively anticipates customer needs. Understands the customer's specific requirements, and uses this to promote AXP products and seeks opportunities to build new and improve existing business. Ensures premium value is delivered. Makes sure the customer experience is positive, effective, and of high quality to continually enhance the American Express brand.

Drives Innovation & Change

Carries out systematic and rational analysis to identify the root cause of problems Is prepared to challenge the status quo and drives innovation through thinking outside the box. Makes informed judgments. Generates creative ideas/solutions.

MAXIMIZE CONTROL | DRIVE SAVINGS | BENEFIT EMPLOYEES | MANAGE GLOBALLY | MAXIMIZE CONTROL | DRIVE SAVINGS | BENEFIT EMPLOYEES | MANAGE GLOBALLY | MAXIMIZE CONTROL | REAL BUSINESS. REAL SOLUTIONS.™

1

CORPORATE SERVICES
EXPENSE MANAGEMENT SOLUTIONS

2

Overview of Leadership Competencies

Builds & Leverages Relationships

Coordinates efforts/resources within and across teams to deliver goals. Recognizes the importance of teamwork to achieve objectives; brings in ideas, information, suggestions and expertise from others outside the immediate team. Builds strong team relationships within and across teams.

Communicates Effectively

Communicates openly and confidently. Influences, and convinces others in a way that results in acceptance and agreement. Shapes conversations to ensure focus and understanding. Speaks frankly, debates at the table, not afterwards – engages in constructive confrontation. Is a supportive listener.

Builds Diverse Talent

Creates a high commitment work environment where people are motivated and encouraged to achieve through empowerment and development. Takes accountability for building a team with diverse leadership and technical skills. Strengthens American Express' reputation as an employer of choice.

Demonstrates Personal Excellence

Acts with integrity. Shows energy and resilience, and maintains commitment in the face of setbacks and obstacles. Keeps difficulties in perspective and remains positive. Understands own strengths and limitations and is focused on self-development. Is authentic, approachable, open and honest.

AMERICAN EXPRESS

MAXIMIZE CONTROL | DRIVE SAVINGS | BENEFIT EMPLOYEES | MANAGE GLOBALLY | MAXIMIZE CONTROL | DRIVE SAVINGS | BENEFIT EMPLOYEES | MANAGE GLOBALLY | MAXIMIZE CONTROL | REAL BUSINESS. REAL SOLUTIONS.℠

Reprinted with permission of American Express, Global Talent.

How did he identify the right competencies? Even though the competencies were not included in the job posting, he knew where to look for them on his own company's Website. *(Note: Sometimes you have to demonstrate resourcefulness to identify the right competencies. More pointers on how to identify competencies—even the "hidden" competencies—are included in Chapter 3.)*

This is the list of competencies used by his company for the position he wanted:

Thought

Creating Innovative Solutions.

Thinking Analytically and Conceptually.

Acting Strategically and Globally.

Results

Driving Results.

Exceeding Customer Expectations.

Risk-Taking.

Acting Decisively.

Relationships

Collaborating and Influencing Others.

Demonstrating Integrity.

Treating People with Respect.

People

Managing Performance.

Developing People.

Managing Change.

---

2. **Think about what you have done that demonstrates expertise or experience with each of the competencies.**

Determine an approach that will work well for you. Are you a linear thinker? If so, consider thinking about what you have done in each position you've held, and then break it down into a list of competencies. If you are not a linear thinker, and it will work more effectively for you to just list things by competency area, use that approach. Take some notes.

3. Develop accomplishment statements for as many of the competencies as you can.

One critical point is to assess your own writing skills and tolerance for frustration. Because you need to use your own time as effectively as possible, you may decide to work with a consultant to develop your accomplishment statements and the rest of the resume. Or you may decide to write it on your own.

The first step in writing your accomplishments is to take the list you've developed in number 2, then brainstorm and write down as many more examples as you can *for each competency*. Get the main points down and try not to worry about the exact wording at this stage.

This is the list the IT manager developed:

Thought   **Creating Innovative Solutions:** Designed and implemented through outsourcing technology development a benchmark tool to be used internally. Tool is now being enhanced for global application to support regional competitive advantage. Led integration of an expanded Web product offering to support multiclient setup for relationship managers. Awarded Global Recognition Award for Excellence for exceeding expectations by identifying innovated solutions for accelerating product launch of Web products globally and establishing processes in each of the regional markets addressing both customer focus and local market requirements.

Thinking Analytically and Conceptually: Awarded Chairman's Award for Achievement by providing solutions and alternatives to accelerate development of product enhancements. Led Six Sigma project; reduced project development cycle time resulting in budget savings and ahead of scheduled rollout.

Acting Strategically and Globally: Awarded Chairman's Award for Achievement by leading implementation of new product line paving the way for increased delivery of electronic reporting to customer. Closely coordinated with international partners to make sure product met local, regional, as well as global requirements. Worked closely with billing process to ensure product P&L supported strategy and revenue targets. Created, reviewed, and negotiated associated documentation for SQP funding request process ensuring that customer needs were addressed.

Results   **Driving Results:** Awarded Global Recognition Award for Excellence for leading team and challenging status quo resulting in successfully implemented product pilot and eventual full product launch on target despite obstacles in economy, security approvals, and requirement changes. Continued migration of legacy product to alternative tools despite poor economic and system performance impacts.

Exceeding Customer Expectations: Redesign of client User Guide material and posted information to Website, making client access to support material much easier.

Risk-Taking: Awarded Global Recognition Award for Excellence for exceeding expectations with risk-taking while keeping customer focus by launching product in local markets through U.S. site when local market system infrastructure would not support launch. Met with many large customers to address their concerns head-on.

Acting Decisively: Made frequent decisions on product changes without initial senior management approval to remain on timelines. Provided communications to ensure ultimate concurrence from senior management.

Relationships   **Collaborating and Influencing Others:** Established new relationship within Amex across function and departments. Designed a process for Supplier Relations Group to receive information directly for contract negotiations. Built new relationship with regional groups and now attend monthly field presentations to keep teams apprised of changes in the markets. Built rapport with technologies, servicing, relationship management, and customers, providing a strong network for servicing and product management to exchange information. Performed product demonstrations/presentation in numerous meetings as well as directly with clients that assured retention of millions of dollars in travel business.

Developing People: Continue to take on additional roles in giving guidance and coaching to peers.

The next step is to try to get more specific and develop well-written accomplishment statements targeted to each of the competencies. Most career consultants agree that strong accomplishment statements include these three components, which are sometimes referred to as P-A-R:

★ Problem or Situation.

★ Action.

★ Result.

(Note: Career consultants may disagree on the order that the three should be presented.)

If you have trouble coming up with specific examples, you might want to talk to a mentor or consultant. When the IT manager had difficulty with the competency "treating people with respect," we suggested that he use examples from when he had worked with a diverse group of people. Here's an example:

◆ Selected to win 2001 Performer Award for accurately assessing market needs in the United States, Asia/Pacific, and Latin America and determining product applications for software.

◆ Recognized for ability to develop effective working relationships with diverse teams/cultures by being asked to attend monthly international relationship manager meetings.

The manager thought of several other accomplishments that were included in his first draft. In most cases, he had to make some decisions—which were the best accomplishments that clearly demonstrated the competencies?

Remember when you are working on your accomplishment statements to write concisely and powerfully. The architect Ludwig Mies van der Rohe is known for building skyscrapers with the design philosophy that "less is more." Less is also more on a resume.

Take a look at Daniel Marrs's competency-based resume on pages 46–47 for more examples of the accomplishments we agreed to include.

 Hint: Read Chapter 5 for more specific ideas about how to write extremely effective competency-based accomplishment statements.

4. **Write the summary section so it emphasizes your experience and strengths related to the key competencies for the position. Include relevant information and personalize the section if there's enough space.**

SUMMARY

Product Development Manager with expertise in travel and card information. Recognized for achieving results by launching Web-enabled product to begin decommissioning legacy products, accelerating implementation of reporting tools in regional markets, and designing/developing database tool for benchmarking travel expenditures. Strengths include building effective working relationships by collaborating with and influencing clients/coworkers and working closely with manager to develop members of team by acting as subject matter expert on travel, card, purchasing, and expense. Innovative, analytical risk-taker with proven track record of developing global solutions. Licensed to fly high-performance multiengine jet aircraft.

Six Sigma Certification: Green Belt, 2002

Technical Certifications: SQL Database, MS Access

Pay attention to several of the ways we made his summary emphasize the competencies his company identified as key for this position.

We included key competencies and synonyms in the actual summary.

- Recognized for achieving results.
- Effective working relationships (in today's legal climate, it is much safer to include the word "working").
- Collaborating with and influencing.
- Develop members of team.
- Innovative.
- Analytical.
- Risk-taker.
- Solutions (similar to results and known to be a current buzzword in his company).

In addition, we included information about his license in flying, Six Sigma certification, and computer skills to further demonstrate his ability to achieve goals and understand technical information.

Summaries are critical to include in the resume because they function as the reader's first impression of your background. The summary sells you to the hiring manager. Does the summary emphasize the right competency-based message to help give you an edge over the competition in getting the interview?

For additional information about how to write strong competency-based summary or profile sections, see Chapter 7.

5. **Determine which competency-based resume format—chronological, functional, direct competency, or combination—best fits your needs. Prepare your first draft of the resume.**

In this situation, the client had been with his company for a number of years and had directly worked for two of the decision-makers he expected to be involved in making the decision about whether he would be given the promotion. They knew him, and they knew his work.

Because the client had a fairly straightforward background and was trying to prepare a resume to help ensure he was selected for an interview for a position that would be a promotion, we decided to help him develop a competency-based chronological resume. In other cases, another competency-based resume format might make more sense. Making the right decision on a resume format is discussed in more detail in Chapter 6.

6. **Remember to include sections on your education and any other specific information relevant to potential employers.**

Be aware that there have been some highly publicized cases of people falsifying their educational credentials in recent years. In this section, it is important to be very careful about details. If employers are going to check the validity of anything on your resume, it will probably be to verify that you received your degree from the school you've identified on your resume.

Make sure that the date of your degree is accurate if you decide to include it on your resume. When to include the year you received your degree and other decision points related to education and other information are discussed in more detail in Chapter 7.

 Hint: In general, most career consultants are encouraging their clients to include graduation dates only when they are recent (within 10 years) to make it harder to discriminate against them based upon their age.

7. **Add additional competency-related accomplishment statements, and if you still have space, other accomplishment statements.**

Determine how your accomplishment statements *fit*. If you know the weightings given to the competencies, try to have that same percentage of accomplishments in each competency area. This kind of information *may* be available to you if you already work for the organization and are interested in a promotion or transfer, or if you are lucky or *savvy* enough to have an "inside" contact.

Check to determine that the number of accomplishments under each section looks reasonable. Think about how long you've been in each job and how related it is to what you want to do next. Deciding the right number of accomplishments to use is covered in Chapters 5 and 8.

Hint: For example, if you are developing a competency-based chronological resume, you should plan to have five to eight accomplishments under your most recent job—unless you've only been in that position for a short time. If you are developing a competency-based functional resume, plan to have roughly three to six accomplishments under each functional area. Occasionally, there is a compelling reason to have more (or less) accomplishments listed in a section, so you will have to use your judgement.

8. **Prioritize competency-related phrases in your summary section and competency-based accomplishments within the appropriate sections of the resume.**

9. **Review and polish your resume. Ask other professionals for input.**

Editing and reviewing the resume are extremely important if you want to come across as professionally as possible. Make sure that the font you use is professional and large enough for managers with poor eyesight to see without reading glasses. Remember that your resume is a work in progress. Always tailor the resume based on competencies for individual positions. More specific suggestions are covered in Chapter 8.

10. **Finalize your resume. Develop an electronic version of the resume with a keyword summary section that includes competencies (and synonyms for competencies) to increase your chance of being selected for an interview when an organization is using screening software.**

Take a look at the resumes we worked with on the next few pages that demonstrates this approach. We included the original resume on page 45 and then followed it with the resume we helped our client develop. You can clearly see the difference using the competency-based method can make. It worked for Dan. And it will work for you.

Remember: This system uses just 10 key steps.
Are you ready to begin?

Original Resume

Daniel Marrs

451 Bonhomme Ave
St. Louis, MO 63105
dan.r.marrs@aexp.com

(314) 954-3950
(314) 599-0000

Objective:

To continue career progression within company by expanding my influence, coordination and directing skills beyond product development and into areas that will challenge and include aspects of management information where my experience and accomplishments will allow opportunity to develop employee resources and processes.

Experience:

American Express, St. Louis, MO   **1992–Present**

1997-Present   *Manager Global Product Development*

I am responsible for directing the global development and management of the following information products for both internal and external users around the globe across card and travel management information service; Reporting Package, Trip Reporting Program, Purchase Tracking program, Card Usage Program, and additional financial and project management programs. These range from PC-based installation to web interactive products.

1995-1997   *Customer Service: Specialist*

I managed development of training database for internal and external classes while at the same time was responsible for the team performance as Customer Service Lead in support. Created Quality Assurance database to ensure effective processes. Provided second level support for domestic and international regions. I was responsible for timely and accurate completion of audit report analysis and customization of client reports based on client need for audit. Implementation of new accounts.

1994-1995   *Customer Service: Consultant*

- Managed support responsibilities as Customer Service Lead for specialized travel reporting tool.
- Provided internal and external client training.
- Instrumental in international rollout of MIS PC Card reporting tools.

1992-1994   *Customer Service: Analyst*

- Responsible for timely/accurate completion of audit report analysis.
- Customization of client reports based on client need for audit.
- Implementation of new MIS accounts.

US Department of Transportation FAA, Wichita Falls, TX   **1980–1992**

Air Traffic Controller

- Radar Approach Control, Remote Radar and Center Certified.

Additional Projects: Created and implemented a simulator program to radically reduce upgrade and certification for Air Traffic Control Operators. Managed individual performance and career development for staff reporting directly to me.

Proficiencies:

Microsoft Project, Microsoft Access, SQL, Microsoft Word, Microsoft Excel

Education:

Air Force Academy; Green Belt Six Sigma Certification

Awards:

2000, 2001 Global Recognition Award for Excellence. 1995, 1999, 2000 Chairman's Award for Achievement
1999, 2000, 2001 Annual Star Performer Award. 1994, 1999, 2001 Letter of Appreciation
1992 Accommodation Award

Competency-Based Resume
DANIEL MARRS

451 Bonhomme Avenue   314.954.3950 / 314.494.853
St. Louis, MO 63105   dan.r.marrs@aexp.cor

SUMMARY

Product Development Manager with expertise in travel and card information. Recognized for achieving results by launching Web-enabled product to begin decommissioning legacy products, accelerating implementation of reporting tools in regional markets, and designing/developing database tool for benchmarking travel expenditures. Strengths include building effective working relationships by collaborating with clients/coworkers, and working closely with manager to develop team members as subject matter expert on travel, card, purchasing and expense. Innovative, analytical risk-taker with proven track record of developing global solutions. Licensed to fly high-performance multiengine jet aircraft.

Six Sigma Certifications: Green Belt, 2002.
Technical Certifications: SQL Database, MS Access.

EXPERIENCE

American Express, St. Louis, MO   **1992–Present**
Company Awards: Global Recognition Award for Excellence (2001, 2000), Chairman's Award for Achievement (2000, 1999, 1995), Annual Star Performer (2001, 2000, 1999), Letter of Appreciation (2001, 1999, 1994).

Manager Global Product Development, 1997–Present
- Recognized with 2001 Global Recognition Award for Excellence by identifying innovative solutions for accelerating global product launch of corporate travel reporting tool to address international customer and regional requirements.
- Awarded 2000 Global Recognition Award for Excellence for leading team and challenging status quo by implementing product pilot/launch on target despite changes in economy and security requirements.
- Received 1999 Chairman's Award for Achievement for providing solutions/alternatives to accelerate development and product testing for new product enhancements; led Six Sigma project to reduce project development cycle time 40% resulting in significant savings and increased client satisfaction.
- Saved $125,000 by contracting and accelerating product development of benchmarking tool by six months; increased timeliness of processing, added industry trend data to system, and contributed to expanding application globally to support regional competitive advantage.
- Successfully migrated 200 corporate clients from legacy products onto alternative reporting tools/solutions despite poor economy and system performance; immediately saved 1,000 hours of employee time with forecasted savings of $1 million once project completed, 2004.
- Exceeded expectations with risk-taking while keeping customer focus by launching product in local markets using U.S. Website when local market system infrastructure would not support launch; saved company $250,000 by taking risk.
- Working closely with Amex professionals from Latin America, Asia Pacific, and Europe; recognized for ability to develop effective working relationships with diverse teams/cultures by being asked to attend monthly international relationship manager meetings.
- Recognized with 2001 Star Performer Award for assessing market needs and determining product applications for new travel reporting tool.
- Won 2000 Star Performer Award by ensuring timely launch for product, being decisive on product changes before communication strategy completed, and communicating daily with key department heads to ensure buy in.

DANIEL MARRS   **Page 2**

American Express (Continued)
Customer Service Specialist, 1995–1997
Customer Service Consultant, 1994–1995

- Received Chairman's Award for Achievement in 1995 by designing and standardizing customer training for new travel information product.
- Organized Information Services User Conference attended by 200 client Travel Managers; won 1995 Star Performer Award.
- Recognized with Letter of Appreciation for retaining business from Big Five accounting firm after receiving feedback from client manager and sales saying customer relationship at risk.
- Met with senior management from unhappy client and built new relationship; developed innovative solutions to manage T&E and created opportunity for $300 million in new business.
- Analyzed needs of 100 clients to develop plan for management information, facilitated report cycle and product demonstrations, training, and issue resolutions; achieved increase in product utilization and understanding of industry trends.

Customer Service Analyst, 1993–1994
Customer Service Operator II, 1992–1993

- Analyzed past practices for monitoring AS400 reliability, formalized recommendation for process/servicing improvements, and ensured system integrity and performance.
- Saved major system outage by effectively responding and communicating with IT management.

U.S. Department of Transportation, Wichita Falls, TX   **1980–1992**
Facility Coordinator, 1990–1992
Air Traffic Control Operator, 1980–1990

- Received Accommodation Award for outstanding performance for improving facility safety rating to excellent with zero incidents for 330,000 flight operations.
- Promoted to facility coordinator for regional operations control, Central-Southwest, U.S., including DFW; helped train NATO pilots and managed crew of 25 air traffic controllers.
- Led design and creation of training certification simulation program; reduced time needed for certifying new Air Traffic Control Operators and upgrading existing certifications by 70%.

EDUCATION

B.A.–Aeronautics, Air Force Academy

Key Points for Chapter 4	
"Excellence is not a singular act, but a habit. You are what you repeatedly do." —Shaquille O'Neal (This quotation is a paraphrase of an older quote by Aristotle)	
Key Questions	**Answers**
What are the benefits of writing a competency-based resume?	Here's a list of the benefits for developing a competency-based resume. Competency-based resumes will: • *Confirm* to the employer that you have the expertise—or competency—they are looking for. • *Improve* your chance of being selected for interviews for the positions that you want. • *Help* you be perceived as more clearly competitive.
Why is it important to follow the steps when you write a competency-based resume?	Following the steps ensures that you will remember to include everything that needs to be included in your competency-based resume.
What are the steps you should follow?	1. Identify competencies for the position. 2. Think about what you have done that demonstrates expertise or experience with each of the competencies. 3. Develop accomplishment statements for as many of the competencies as you can. 4. Write the summary section so it emphasizes your experience and strengths related to the key competencies for the position. Include relevant information and personalize the section if there's enough space. 5. Determine which competency-based resume format—chronological, functional, direct competency, or combination—best fits your needs, and prepare your first draft of the resume. 6. Remember to include sections on your education and any other specific information relevant to potential employers. 7. Add additional competency-related accomplishment statements, and if you still have space, other accomplishment statements. 8. Prioritize competency-related phrases in your summary section and competency-based accomplishments within the appropriate sections of the resume. 9. Review and polish your resume. Ask other professionals for input. 10. Finalize your resume. Develop an electronic version of the resume with a keyword summary section.
Why is the summary section of the resume important?	**Summaries are critical.** They function as the reader's first impression of your background and highlight how you meet the most critical competencies for the position. View the summary as an opportunity to sell your background to the employer. Take the time to put some effort into writing it.
What about my education? Should I include dates?	Include graduation dates only when they are recent (within 10 years). Be careful about including dates. If you include them, they must be exact because that is how your education is verified—by graduation date or last date attended.

Chapter 5

Develop Strong Competency-Based Accomplishment Statements

When an author writes a good murder mystery, it is critical that we've been given enough clues—provided enough evidence—so that we are convinced the detective has caught the right killer by the end of the book. We need to be convinced the detective has done the research, examined the evidence, and provided evidence strong enough to convict the suspect.

The best resumes provide relevant, specific evidence that the person is highly competent in the areas needed by the employer. It is important to remember that:

★ Many resumes get moved to the bottom of the pile if they don't seem to *fit* the position.

★ Most people make the decision if your resume *fits* before finishing reading the resume.

★ In today's high-tech world, screening software reduces the number of resumes the human resources professional or hiring manager needs to go through.

Specific evidence shown on the resume is extremely important in helping the decision-makers make the right decision to invite you in for an interview.

Remember that we routinely hire inspectors to make sure the houses we buy are as structurally sound as the sellers indicate. When college admissions officers made the brilliant decision to accept us at their universities, they did so (and we're convinced still do so) based upon the quality of our grades, our high school, our test scores, our recommendations, and our essays.

Major decisions, including who gets hired and who gets promoted, are almost always made by someone who seriously considers the evidence and makes their best judgment about who is innocent or guilty, what problems we might face, if we are going to be admitted at a university—and if we are going to receive a job offer. The evidence the decision-maker looks at helps them determine the outcome.

With employment decisions, the key is who is perceived as the best qualified. The decision-maker's perception can be influenced by his or her own past experience, the verbal or nonverbal communication skills of the candidate, and other related issues—and is rarely based on "just the facts." Most people making these decisions, though, genuinely try to do the best that they can do for the organization they are recruiting for. They are professionals; they like to think that most of their recommendations are based upon sound, professional reasoning.

How can we get the person making the decision to realize that you are the best qualified?

When you are getting ready to write a competency-based resume, remember to ask yourself, "How do I present my background in a way that increases the chance that the decision-maker will perceive me as being the best qualified?"

It is important to remember that in a competency-based organization, your competencies—your knowledge, skills, and abilities—will help determine the perception of how qualified you are for any position.

> **"Experience is not what happens to you; it's what you do with what happens to you."**
>
> —Aldous Huxley

In this chapter we're going to show you how to present your background in a way that showcases your competencies. And we're going to encourage you to consider trying to write your resume in a new, more interesting way that will increase the chance that decision-makers will read the whole resume!

More and more organizations are using recruiting software today to help them reduce the number of resumes they have to review by using keywords or tag words. But it is important to remember that recruiters or managers still go through the remaining smaller pile and decide who to bring in for interviews. By including competencies on your resume, especially in the keyword section, you increase the chance that the recruiting software will select your resume, and the human resources professional will decide you deserve an interview.

We want you to be able to help manage the decision-maker's perspective by writing accomplishment statements that show how competent you are in the areas that their organization cares about. In other words, you are going to give them the clues in the resume and help them see the evidence that *you are the best fit* for their position by emphasizing *your* accomplishments that match what *they* are looking for. We will also review the basics to write an effective electronic resume using keywords or tag words in Chapter 6.

In this chapter, we encourage you to:

1. Review the competencies identified by the organization (or selected as "most likely" by you).

2. Write strong accomplishment statements to prove that you have experience and achievements in each of those competency areas.

For our examples in this chapter, we're going to focus on positions in accounting, human resources, and sales, because even if you are most interested in another area, almost all of us know something about these functional areas.

Let's start with identifying the competencies. If you are looking at the list of competencies identified in an advertisement by the employer, you still need to exercise some judgment and ask yourself if the list makes sense for your professional area—or if perhaps something critical has been left out.

Accounting

We found an advertisement on Monster.com on March 2, 2004, for a Staff Accountant for Carlson Companies, Inc.

Carlson Companies is one of the largest privately held companies in the United States and was included in *Fortune* magazine's 2002 list of "The 100 Best Companies to Work For" and *Working Mother* magazine's 2001 to 2004 lists of "The 100 Best Companies for Working Mothers." The company is based in Minneapolis, Minnesota, and is the corporate headquarters for Radisson Hotels & Resorts, T.G.I. Friday's, Carlson Wagonlit Travel, Carlson Marketing Group, and other well-known brands and services that collectively employ approximately 190,000 people in more than 140 countries.

The online advertisement clearly identified 10 competencies for the position:

1. Focus on the Customer.

2. Build Strong Relationships.

3. Influence Others.

4. Develop Self and Others.

5. Share Information.

6. Drive for Continuous Improvement.

7. Drive for Results.

8. Analyze and Make Decisions.

9. Apply Professional, Product, and Technical Expertise.

10. Attend to Detail.

Human Resources

Sears posted an advertisement for a Human Resources Consultant in Chicago on Monster.com on April 3, 2004. Sears, Roebuck and Co., is headquartered in Chicago, Illinois, and is a leading retailer providing merchandise and related services in the United States and Canada.

In Sears's advertisement, competencies are divided into three categories: Leadership Principles, HR Core Competencies, and Job-Specific Technical Competencies.

Leadership Principles

Customer Focus.

Change Management.

Drive for Results.

Teamwork.

Performance Management.

Diversity/Inclusiveness.

HR Core Competencies

Strategic Business Perspective.

People Practices Design/Execution.

Fact-Based Problem-Solving.

Project and Process Orientation.

Coaching and Influencing Others.

Personal Impact.

Job-Specific Technical Competencies

Employment Practices.

Conducting Investigations.

Conflict Resolution.

Negotiation.

Relationship Building.

Sales

After reviewing several advertisements for sales positions, we decided to choose the online ad run on March 24, 2004, by StorageTek for a Disk Storage Product Sales Specialist in New York City.

StorageTek, located just outside Boulder, Colorado, specializes in delivering innovative storage solutions to manage and protect critical information for businesses. The company has 7,000 employees worldwide and was listed on *Fortune* magazine's list of "America's Most Admired Companies in the Computer Peripherals" category in 2002, 2003, and 2004.

The general competencies identified in the ad for the position are:

1. Customer Focus.

2. Interpersonal Savvy.

3. Technical Learning.

4. Perseverance.

5. Business Acumen.

6. Dealing With Ambiguity.

7. Presentation.

8. Organizing.

9. Negotiating.

After reviewing the general competencies list, it is clear that "achieving results" (or an equivalent term) is missing, and that is extremely important—actually critical— to be successful in *any* sales position. Because we know how key that competency is, we would add "achieving results" to the competency list. We recommend reading the complete advertisement to see what else could be considered a competency but is listed in another part of the advertisement.

Always remember to ask yourself if the list you are working with hits the major requirements to be successful on the job.

To be successful with your resume, you may have to do some intelligence work. We can give you some ideas in this book about how to do it, but in the end, you need to take responsibility, use your own resourcefulness, and think!

Technical competencies listed for the position:

1. In-depth knowledge of company/competitor products sufficient to provide leadership in developing storage solutions and customer presentations.

2. Demonstrated knowledge of sales methodologies and account management.

3. Demonstrated success in account planning and development of sales strategies.

4. Demonstrated ability to analyze/rate sales opportunities.

5. Proven ability to develop accurate forecasts.

6. Technical, competitor, and industry knowledge.

7. Proven ability to achieve results and exceed goals.

8. Able to close business while dealing with complex, challenging conditions.

In sales, understanding the product or service and being able to communicate well enough to convince people to buy your product are critical steps to achieving those results—making the sale. You need to be able to demonstrate to the decision-maker through how you write about your accomplishments that you have demonstrated competency in these areas.

Basic Tips for Writing Accomplishment Statements

1. **Write your accomplishments in a way that demonstrates expertise and shows relevant experience for each of the competencies the company is looking for.**

Let's take the competency "Drive for Results." If you are a salesperson, what is the best clue that you are strong in this competency area? The answer is fairly simple: you've achieved significant results. If you have been a consistently top-ranked salesperson, you obviously have a strong drive for results.

So your strongest accomplishment statements should talk about the sales awards you have won, how quickly you made your first sale, or how you overcame an obstacle to close a significant sale.

If you haven't achieved at the highest level, develop a statement that sounds as strong as possible for what you have accomplished. For example, you could say: "Recognized by manager for closing $300,000 in sales in first two months at company." (You may not have closed any sales in the next 10 months, but the statement is still true!)

These are some accomplishment statements we developed for one sales professional we worked with that directly provide evidence of his "Drive for Results":

Recognized for exceeding sales goals at IBM and Lexmark with:

- Lexmark's Winner's Circle for top 2 percent of U.S. sales professionals.
- Sales Director Award: top-ranked sales performer in U.S. Healthcare Division (two consecutive years), first back-to-back Sales Director Award winner in the North American sales organization.
- Account Executive of the Year, three years; and of the Quarter, 14 quarters.
- Area Systems Engineer of the Quarter, four quarters.
- IBM 100% Club and Systems Engineering Symposium.
- Printing and Publishing Specialist of the Year, two years.
- Grew revenues in new healthcare territory to $2.6 million in only two years.
- Increased sales to Shell Oil Co. and Texaco from $500,000 to $2 million in two years.
- Improved IBM printer product market share in territory from 9 percent to 20 percent in 22 months.

2. **Remember to include information that explains the situation (or problem), action, and result.**

Before you start writing the accomplishment statement, take the time to describe what the situation was or what the problem was that you solved. What action did you take? What was the result? How did the organization or your department benefit from what you did?

Here's an example from a fairly senior-level accounting manager's resume. This accomplishment statement demonstrates the manager is strong in the competencies "Drive for Results" *and* "Drive for Continuous Improvement."

> - Managed 75-percent increase in AP and AR volume without increasing 15-employee staff; streamlined work processes and provided incentives to improve individual productivity.

This statement would be even stronger if you included specific numbers to enable the reader to know what a 75-percent increase in volume actually meant.

> **For every competency you have, you should know and be able to communicate how it will achieve results that matter to the company.**

The best accomplishment statements will include the situation/problem (75-percent increase in work volume), action (streamlined processes and provided incentives), and result (managed without increasing staff). The order that you cover these three pieces should depend upon which you decide is the most critical to the person who will be reviewing your resume.

Some career consultants believe in following the same order with each statement; others believe in varying the order to emphasize the most important piece first, or simply as a way to keep the reader's interest.

3. **Start each statement with action verbs. Vary the words you use.**

Remember to begin every accomplishment statement with an action verb. Try to use different words to help your reader stay interested. Make the words as strong and precise as possible.

In one resume workshop, every participant had implemented at least three things. The word "implemented" implies that you had a lower-level role and just followed through on what someone else developed, created, planned, or decided to do. Did you play a significant role in the project or did you *just* "implement" it?

Always go for the highest level that you can when you are deciding how much credit to claim. Modesty may be a virtue in other parts of your life, but it is not a virtue when you are writing your resume—or in your career. Take credit for the things you have accomplished.

Action Words			
Use any of the following action words to add impact and energy to your resume.[1]			
Accomplished	Detected	Instructed	Purchased
Achieved	Determined	Integrated	Recommended
Adjusted	Developed	Interpreted	Reduced
Administered	Devised	Invented	Referred
Advised	Diagnosed	Justified	Regulated
Analyzed	Directed	Lectured	Reorganized
Approved	Discovered	Led	Replaced
Arranged	Distributed	Lobbied	Reported
Assisted	Edited	Maintained	Represented
Budgeted	Eliminated	Managed	Researched
Built	Enlarged	Modified	Restored
Calculated	Established	Motivated	Reviewed
Charted	Evaluated	Negotiated	Revised
Compared	Examined	Obtained	Scheduled
Compiled	Expanded	Operated	Selected
Completed	Flagged	Ordered	Served
Composed	Formed	Organized	Sold
Conducted	Formulated	Overhauled	Solved
Consolidated	Founded	Performed	Studied
Constructed	Gathered	Persuaded	Supervised
Consulted	Generated	Planned	Supplied
Controlled	Guided	Prepared	Systematized
Conceptualized	Headed	Presided	Taught
Coordinated	Identified	Processed	Tested
Counseled	Improved	Produced	Traced
Created	Increased	Programmed	Trained
Decreased	Initiated	Projected	Translated
Delivered	Inspected	Promoted	Updated
Designated	Installed	Proposed	Utilized
Designed	Instituted	Provided	Won
			Wrote

4.　Target your audience by using language they will understand.

Who are you writing this resume for? The hiring manager? The human resources manager? The recruiter?

Our answer: anyone who could be involved in the decision to give you an interview, or eventually a job offer. Be careful about using language that is too technical or includes too much jargon. Don't be too simplistic. Don't be too casual either.

5.　Give specific examples to support your experience with each competency.

Include specific details when you are writing accomplishment statements. If you keep things vague and general, your credibility isn't as strong as if you go into enough details to prove that you actually have experience in a particular area. Don't bury them with the details, just give enough to provide evidence that you've done the things you've claimed credit for.

Go through the list of competencies for the position you are interested in—one at a time. Ask yourself, "What have I done that proves I have some competence in each area?" At this stage, don't eliminate anything; write down everything that you can think of under each competency area. Then try to go back and turn the "evidence" into more polished accomplishment statements.

6.　Quantify your example whenever possible.

The person reading your resume needs to be able to understand how significant your accomplishment is. Compare these two examples:

> ■ Managed human resources department for division.

> ■ Directed human resources for 1,100-employee division of Fortune 500 company; directly supervised seven human resources professionals and three clerks and managed budget of $1.5 million.

Do you see the difference? By including the number of employees and the size of the budget, you are providing the decision-maker with the evidence that you can do the job. Be positive when you are making a decision about which number to choose; always choose the statistic or the number that is the most impressive, while still being realistic. Don't be too modest.

It is perfectly acceptable to round larger numbers. Round up when it will strengthen your case; round down when it won't.

7.　Say as much as you can in as few words as you can.

This tip applies to the complete resume. It is extremely important to be as concise as possible.

We want to provide as much hard-hitting evidence that you match the employer's needs as possible in the space that we have, whether it is a one- or two-page resume. This rationale is why you almost never see complete sentences on a well-written resume—they aren't a good use of the space.

Make sure that every word adds something to the content. Try to eliminate words such as "various" and "numerous" that don't tell us anything new. For example, saying that you worked in various facilities doesn't tell the reader as much as if you are specific and claim "five facilities." If for some reason you can't be specific, just simply say "facilities," because using the plural does tell us that you are talking about more than one!

Remove words such as "that," "the," "a," and "an," which may not add anything to your content.

When you are using quantitative examples, make a judgment call as to what is the most powerful way to say something. Is "one in four" more impressive than "25 percent"? It depends on what point you are trying to make!

Remember that it is better to round numbers or percentages if you are not absolutely sure than it is to repeatedly use terms that sound hesitant such as "approximately," the "+" sign after a number, "around," "under," "less than," "above," or "around."

8. **If your best example under an individual competency isn't a particularly strong accomplishment, then try to write it so that it sounds as strong as possible.**

For many people it is often hard to identify a significant accomplishment. In some cases, you are being too modest. You need to push yourself to think about it more in-depth.

But in other cases, there may be good reasons that you cannot come up with something strong, such as having only been in an assignment for a few months or supporting others on a project and not taking the lead. What can you do in these situations?

Take as much credit as you can for the outcome without lying . Here's an example. The accountant originally wrote:

> ■ Worked on PeopleSoft transition team.

After talking with her and asking her to be more specific, we identified three competencies related to working on the PeopleSoft project. We decided to focus on what she'd done related to "Sharing Information," "Drive for Results," and "Apply Professional, Product, and Technical Expertise." Then we wrote:

> - Selected to represent accounting department on five-person corporate team evaluating and recommending PeopleSoft modules; coordinated department activity and prepared weekly updates for 60 employees in department to ensure smooth transition.
> - Recognized for successfully managing PeopleSoft project under budget by senior management with outstanding employee award.

9. After you've written competency-based accomplishment statements, add other accomplishments to your list.

After reviewing the list of relevant competencies for the position you are interested in, consider what else you've done that provides evidence that you will be successful in the position. Read the rest of the advertisement, company literature, and the Website to see what other things the organization might be looking for; develop accomplishment statements about things you have done that can prove you can do these "other things."

Focus first on the organization's needs before you begin to ask yourself the question "What is my biggest accomplishment on the job?" This is one of the biggest differences in the competency-based resume approach. **It isn't all about you; it is about you getting the best opportunity because you've focused on their needs first.**

10. Make sure you have included keywords in your resume.

A high percentage of larger organizations are using recruiting software to help reduce the time that human resources professionals need to screen the resumes that come in. In Chapter 6, we'll talk more about writing electronic competency-based resumes that include a keyword summary section.

Even in your regular Microsoft Word resume, though, you should plan on including the words that someone might identify as key to being successful in your professional area. These words should be embedded in the resume—in accomplishment statements and in the summary section of the resume. Remember to include competencies, and synonyms for the competencies, when you are thinking about keywords. For example, you might talk about "achieving results" in one statement and "reaching a goal" in another.

11. When you realize your best examples in a particular competency area are weak, do the best that you can for now, and then move on.

Try to come up with the best, most relevant experience you can to prove that you're qualified, or competent, in each of the competency areas.

When you can't identify any substantial evidence to prove that you have experience, or the right level of experience, with a particular competency, recognize that you've just found a competency gap, note it, and move on. We'll talk more about how to bridge and overcome the competency gaps in Chapter 14.

Is there an easy way to get some accomplishment statements written down *quickly*?

The most difficult part of writing a resume is compiling and writing accomplishment statements, so here are some tips to get you started if you're in a hurry.

First, look again at the action verbs listed on page 56.

Second, categorize them under the competencies you have already listed for your target position.

Third, write your accomplishment in the standard resume format that always starts with an action verb. State clearly what you accomplished.

> Here are a few questions that will help you get started writing your accomplishment statements.
>
> Answer these questions:
>
> ☆ What did I do? Use an *action* verb to start every accomplishment statement. (A = Action)
>
> ☆ What problem was solved or what situation did I help resolve?
> (P = Problem)
>
> ☆ What was the result(s) of my action: How did it benefit the organization? (R = Result)
>
> Write as many of these as you can for each competency. Then add the grammar, punctuation, and tone.
>
> (*Note: You can also list the result first, but remember to always start with an action verb.*)

Fourth, prioritize your accomplishments by ranking the ones that best target the competencies the organization desires in order of importance to the organization you want to work for.

You may find that after writing an accomplishment statement, it fits and sells your experience much better under another competency.

Check to determine that the number of accomplishments under each section looks reasonable. Think about how long you've been in each job and how related the accomplishments are to what you want to do next.

Key Points for Chapter 5	
"Experience is one thing you can't get for nothing." —Oscar Wilde	
Key Questions	**Answers**
What is recruiting software and how are keywords used?	More organizations are using recruiting software to help reduce the time spent by human resources reviewing resumes. The software identifies the number of *hits* on keywords or tag words and submits the names for review. Your job is to identify the keywords and include them in your resume as often as possible while still focusing on the competencies.
How can I make my accomplishment statements better?	Develop a statement that sounds as strong as possible for what you have accomplished. For example, don't use "implemented" when you can use "directed," "organized," "developed." "Implemented" sounds like you just followed another person's directions.
Why are results so important?	**Results give hard facts that you actually accomplished something of value.** Remember, employers want to know how you are going to help them be successful. You can do this by: • Improving processes. • Saving time. • Solving problems and developing ways to prevent them from happening again. • Having new ideas for developing, improving, or selling products or services. **For every competency you have, you should know how it would achieve results.**
Why does each accomplishment statement have to begin with an action verb?	• It provides energy and action to what you do. • It makes it easier for the reviewer to quickly determine what you know how to do when skimming your resume. • It is the style used for resumes.
How do I know what words to include in my resume to appeal to the target organization?	First, think about the competencies you are trying to get across. Go to the organization's Website or read any publication it produces. You will be able to see what terminology it uses and how sophisticated its documents are. You will also be able to sense the tone and style the organization prefers. Is it formal, energetic, or highly technical? Watch for too much jargon or being too technical. Remember, certain people reviewing your resume may not know the terminology for that particular position.
How do I add credibility to my accomplishment statements?	Quantify your example whenever possible. It adds credibility and helps the employer see how you can make them succeed.
Why is less more?	Less is more because your resume should send a message that is focused and precise. You need to make it easy to quickly review it.

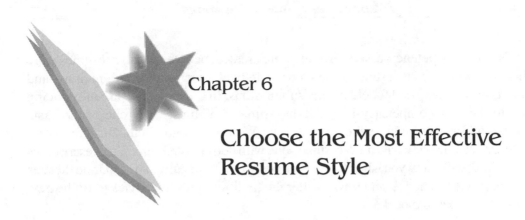

Chapter 6

Choose the Most Effective Resume Style

Throughout this book, we've talked about the importance of understanding what the employer is looking for before beginning to write your resume. Deciding what resume style to use is also extremely important if you want the employer to easily recognize that you are a match for the position.

Most of us make decisions every day that help determine the way we are perceived. Should we wear a business suit or dress business casual for a meeting with a new customer? The choices we make about the clothes we wear *can* influence other people's decisions about:

★ Buying our product.

★ Giving us a key assignment.

★ Hiring us after conducting the interview.

Clark Kent, for example, knows when to keep his glasses on and when to wear his cape. It may be just a little harder to find a phone booth these days, but we are confident that when Metropolis needs a superhero, he can figure out where to change his clothes.

How you look matters. How your resume looks matters too—it can help you get an interview or knock you out of the race.

If you want to be hired as a superhero, your resume needs to look like it belongs to Superman, not Clark Kent. In this chapter, we'll review the strengths of the three basic resume styles: chronological, functional, and direct competency. We'll give you examples of how each resume type can be written the competency-based resume way. The main question is which resume type will work the best for you? Which situations might cause you to choose a different resume style?

Then we'll talk about how to turn these competency-based resumes into electronic resumes. What are the most important things you need to do to make your electronic resume successful when it is sent to a potential employer?

Before competency-based resumes were created, people creating resumes were choosing which resume style to use—chronological, functional, combination—and one style was modified for electronic submissions. In this book, we are introducing you to the new competency-based style resume, which uses any one of the basic formats and adds the competency-based focus. We also are introducing the direct competency resume, which is a new resume style with definite strengths. The descriptions that follow will show you when to use each style, how your particular situation dictates the best style to choose, and how to alter the traditional resume styles to fit the new competency-based model.

Chronological Resumes

Competency-based chronological resumes look very similar to traditional chronological resumes. The main difference is in the content: the summary and the accomplishment statements are written the competency-based way. Employers will just simply think that your resume is well written and that you have the "right" background for the position.

Chronological resumes simply list accomplishments under each position beginning with your current job, so they can be a good choice for people who have always worked in their field, have no interruptions in work experience, and have received no demotions.

A chronological resume is very effective with traditional companies and organizations because it is what they are the most used to seeing. **A competency-based chronological resume is even more effective with these companies because it** *looks* **traditional** *and* **shows them, through the way it is written, that you have the competencies the organization needs.**

Functional Resumes

Competency-based functional resumes are different than regular functional resumes because the summary and accomplishment statements target competencies. Like in the competency-based chronological resume, the summary and accomplishment statements are written the competency-based way.

Functional resumes list accomplishments by functions, not by job titles. Because the work history is included later in the resume, functional resumes put the emphasis on accomplishments, not on your work history.

Using a functional resume can be an extremely good choice for people who have interruptions in their work history, have been demoted, have changed fields, or want to de-emphasize that they worked for an employer in the news, such as Martha Stewart Omnimedia. Functional resumes also work well for consultants because they can emphasize their experience in particular areas for potential clients or employers.

Direct Competency Resumes

Direct competency resumes are the newest resume style, and they have a different look. In a direct competency resume, accomplishments are listed by competency. The summary and the accomplishment statements are written the competency-based way, similar to the other resume styles.

Using a direct competency resume can be a particularly good choice for people to consider if they are already working for an organization such as IBM or American Express that is committed to managing its people using competency-based systems. This resume type will allow you to showcase your accomplishments in each competency area your manager or director is being told they need to care about.

Direct competency resumes can be used to apply for new positions or assignments within organizations that use competency-based systems. You can provide your manager with an updated direct competency resume before receiving your performance appraisal to ensure your manager is aware of your accomplishments in each competency area.

If you've done your research and talked to professionals within the organization you want to work for, you may find that there is an organization or a particular manager that would like the direct resume competency approach. **Even though many managers and human resources professionals are not as used to this style because it is new, we expect that this resume style will become increasingly popular in the next few years.**

 Hint: Once you have identified the employer's needs, and considered your own history, you can always combine some different elements from the three main resume styles to develop a resume that will meet your own needs. This is called a combination resume. Some examples are included in Chapter 11.

Electronic Resumes

Electronic resumes include:

* A resume written in Word and sent via e-mail.

* Developing your own Website with your resume posted.

* Posting your resume on a job search Website such as Monster.com or CareerBuilder.com.

* An ASCII (American Standard Code for Information Interchange) resume requested by an employer.

In other words, electronic resumes include any resume that is created online and sent to others over the Internet.

Look through the examples included in this chapter. You'll be able to see why certain resume styles might be more effective for you. Any competency-based resume can become an electronic resume by following the basic steps used to create any other electronic resume.

One of the major differences is the addition of the keyword summary, which is included to enable the recruiting software used by many employers to pick up that your background matches what the employer is looking for. Remember to include your key competencies in your keyword summary, and list them early in that section.

Once you have completed writing your resume the competency-based way, one good source for learning how to turn it into an electronic resume is Rebecca Smith's *Electronic Resumes & Online Networking* (Career Press, 2000).

Other Key Points on Resume Style

Each of the resume styles shown in this chapter will be more effective than traditional resumes because in every instance the first thing the writer does is consider the employer's needs. Depending on the employer's needs and how well your experience and background matches the position, you may decide to set up your resume using more than one format, or a combination.

Competency-Based Chronological Resume

JEFFREY K. OLDHAM
5011 Red Bridge Drive
Houston, TX 77087
(281) 858-0130
jkoldham2@swbell.net

SUMMARY

District Sales Manager with expertise in business development, solution sales, and technology. Significant experience in new product marketing: product launch and marketing strategy, strategic alliance building, project management, and consultative selling. Skilled at relationship building, channel and OEM sales, contract negotiations, and closing sales. Consistent top performer with record of achieving results, generating revenue, exceeding sales quotas, and delivering exceptional customer service. Excellent interpersonal, organizational, presentation, and writing skills.

WORK HISTORY

CONSULTANT   **2002–2003**

ECG CORPORATION   **2000–2001**
Director, Business Development, 2000–2001
Senior Program Manager, 2000
- Proposed first company-wide print and document strategy with expected savings of $20 million per year.
- Developed sales/marketing campaign awarded national quality award based on Six Sigma criteria.
- Worked with key departments to define technology needs and product development courses, market positioning, network deployment, and partner activities.
- Developed marketing strategy for "sell through" and "sell with" activities between company and preferred technology vendor.

LEXMARK INTERNATIONAL, INC.   **1992–2000**
Senior Consultant, Education and Government Sales, 2000
Special Assistant to Director, Healthcare Sales, 1999–2000
- Selected for Winner's Circle for top 2% of U.S. sales professionals.
- Named Account Executive of the Year, three years, and of the Quarter, 14 quarters.
- Sold one million custom-built inkjet printers after identifying partnership opportunity with Micron.
- Managed major client business engagements across U.S. to maximize healthcare team revenue; exceeded $6 million revenue goal in five months.
- Recognized in 1999 for achieving highest revenues of first-year sales managers in 1998 while working in previous position.

JEFFREY K. OLDHAM   Page 2

WORK HISTORY (Continued)

LEXMARK INTERNATIONAL, INC.
District Sales Manager, 1997–1999
- Managed team responsible for $12 million national purchase agreement with Columbia/HCA.
- Coached sales and technical support team to develop more innovative sales strategies; increased sales 20% annually per territory.
- Facilitated team of 12 employees to develop "Business Advisor," CD-based consulting tool for U.S. sales force; exceeded functionality and stayed under budget.
- Mentored 11 new hires on sales team; developed, implemented, and tracked results of marketing and sales strategies for team.
- Coordinated team introducing first global 24 by 7 non-stop service and parts delivery offering for NCR.
- Convinced clinical and IT managers to purchase platform upgrades despite competition from onsite vendor; managed rollout at County Hospital District.
- Recognized for successfully managing 11 sales/technical/administrative employees selling printing equipment/services to healthcare customers in 23-state region.

Senior Program Manager, Strategic Alliances, 1996
- Won Sales Director Award as top-ranked sales performer in U.S. Healthcare division, two consecutive years.
- Worked as key member of team developing marketing campaign and presentations to introduce *total cost of printing* concept to customers.
- Managed key project improving customer satisfaction rating from 67% to 95%.

Senior Account Executive, 1994–1996
Account Systems Engineer/ National Account Executive, 1992–1993
- Grew revenues in new healthcare territory to $2.6 million in two years.

IBM CORPORATION   **1987–1992**
Account Systems Engineer, 1990–1992
Printing and Desktop Publishing Specialist, 1988–1990
Dealer Account Representative, National Distribution Division, 1987–1988
- Selected for IBM 100% Club.
- Improved IBM printer market share in territory from 9% to 20% in two years.

EDUCATION

Bachelor of Business Administration, Marketing, Magna cum Laude
University of Houston, Houston, Texas

Competency-Based Functional Resume

JEFFREY K. OLDHAM
5011 Red Bridge Drive
Houston, TX 77087
(281) 858-0130
jkoldham2@swbell.net

SUMMARY

District Sales Manager with track record of achieving results in business development, solution sales, and technology. Significant experience in new product marketing: product launch and marketing strategy, strategic alliance building, project management, and consultative selling. Skilled at relationship building, channel and OEM sales, contract negotiations, and closing sales. Consistent top performer with history of generating revenue, exceeding sales quotas and performance objectives, and delivering exceptional customer service. Excellent presentation, interpersonal, and written communication skills.

ACCOMPLISHMENTS

Sales Awards/Results
- Recognized for exceeding sales goals at IBM and Lexmark with:
  - Lexmark's Winner's Circle for top 2% of U.S. sales professionals.
  - Sales Director Award: top-ranked sales performer in U.S. Healthcare division (two consecutive years), first back-to-back Sales Director Award winner in the North American sales organization.
  - Account Executive of the Year, three years; and of the Quarter, 14 quarters.
  - IBM 100% Club.
- Grew revenues in new healthcare territory to $2.6 million in two years.
- Increased sales to Shell and Texaco from $500,000 to $2 million in 22 months.
- Improved IBM printer market share in territory from 9% to 20% in two years.

Technical Sales/Consulting
- Identified opportunity and delivered OEM product proposal to Micron for Lexmark to build printers; sold one million inkjet printers after negotiating contract.
- Sold printers, networking, electronic forms, consulting services, and bundled desktop publishing to healthcare, corporate, education, and government customers.
- Convinced clinical and IT managers to purchase platform upgrades despite existing on-site competitor; managed rollout at County Hospital District.

Sales Management
- Managed 11 sales, technical support, and administrative employees selling printing equipment and services to healthcare customers in 23 states in Eastern U.S.
- Achieved highest revenues of first-year sales managers; ranked in top 10% of sales managers in employee satisfaction ratings, 2000.
- Directed team closing $12 million national agreement with Columbia/HCA.

ACCOMPLISHMENTS (Continued)

Project Management

- Proposed print/document strategy with savings of $20 million per year.
- Managed CRM project with customer satisfaction improvement from 67% to 95%.
- Delivered "Business Printer Advisor," CD-based "consulting" tool for U.S. sales force. Exceeded functional objectives while achieving ahead-of-schedule delivery.
- Developed sales/marketing campaign; awarded national quality award based on Six Sigma criteria.

Marketing and Business Development

- Developed, implemented, and tracked results of marketing and sales strategies for team; mentored 11 team members.
- Coached sales and technical support team to develop more innovative marketing and sales strategies increasing sales 20% per year per territory.
- Consulted with key departments to define technology and product development needs, customer acquisition, market positioning, and partner activities.
- Selected to work on team developing marketing campaign and presentations to introduce total cost of printing concept to customers.

WORK HISTORY

CONSULTANT   2002–2003

ECG CORPORATION   2000–2001
Director, Business Development, 2000–2001
Senior Program Manager, Strategic Alliances, 2000

LEXMARK INTERNATIONAL, INC.   1992–2000
Senior Consultant, Education and Government Sales, 2000
Special Assistant to Director, Healthcare Sales, 1999–2000
District Sales Manager, 1997–1999
Senior Program Manager, Strategic Alliances, 1996
Senior Account Executive, 1994–1996
Account Systems Engineer/National Account Executive, 1992–1993

INTERNATIONAL BUSINESS MACHINES CORPORATION   1987–1992
Account Systems Engineer, 1990–1992
Printing and Desktop Publishing Specialist, 1988–1990
Dealer Account Representative, 1987–1988

EDUCATION

Bachelor of Business Administration, Marketing, Magna cum Laude
University of Houston, Houston, Texas

Direct Competency Resume

JEFFREY K. OLDHAM
5011 Red Bridge Drive
Houston, TX 77087
(281) 858-0130
jkoldham2@swbell.net

SUMMARY

District Sales Manager with expertise in business development, solution sales, and technology. Significant experience in new product marketing: product launch and marketing strategy, strategic alliance building, project management, and consultative selling. Skilled at relationship building, channel and OEM sales, contract negotiations, and closing sales. Consistent top performer with record of achieving results, generating revenue, exceeding sales quotas, and delivering exceptional customer service. Excellent interpersonal, organizational, presentation and writing skills.

KEY COMPETENCIES

Achieving Results
- Recognized for exceeding sales goals at IBM and Lexmark with:
  - Lexmark's Winner's Circle for top 2% of U.S. sales professionals.
  - Sales Director Award as top ranked sales performer in U.S. Healthcare division, two consecutive years.
  - Account Executive of the Year, three years.
  - Area Systems Engineer of the Quarter, four quarters.
  - IBM 100% Club.
- Achieved highest revenues of first-year sales managers; grew revenues in new healthcare territory to $2.6 million in two years.
- Increased sales to Shell and Texaco from $500,000 to $2 million in two years.
- Developed sales and marketing campaign awarded national quality award based on Six Sigma criteria.

Customer Focus
- Ranked in top 10% of all sales managers in employee satisfaction ratings, 1998.
- Convinced clinical and IT managers to purchase platform upgrades despite competition from onsite vendor; managed rollout at County Hospital District.
- Recognized for quality of customer service while working as key member of team introducing total cost of printing concept to customers.
- Managed CRM project with customer satisfaction rating improving from 67% to 95%.

Interpersonal Skills
- Managed 11 sales, technical support, and administrative employees selling printing equipment and services to healthcare customers in 23 states in Eastern U.S.
- Coached sales and technical support team to develop more innovative sales strategies; increased sales 20% annually per territory.
- Facilitated teambuilding and strategy sessions to ensure team stayed focused on closing $12 million national purchase agreement with Columbia/HCA.

KEY COMPETENCIES (Continued)

Organization
- Coordinated team introducing first global 24 by 7 non-stop service and parts delivery offering for NCR, improved corporate service marketing campaign.
- Organized major client business opportunities across U.S. to maximize healthcare team revenue; exceeded $6 million goal for incremental revenue in five months.

Technical Expertise
- Developed sales methodologies and managed accounts for technical departments to define technology needs, product development courses, market positioning, network deployment, and partner activities.
- Planned and implemented sales/marketing campaign; awarded national quality award based on Six Sigma criteria.

WORK HISTORY

CONSULTANT   2002–2003

ECG CORPORATION   2000–2001
Director, Business Development, 2000–2001
Senior Program Manager, Strategic Alliances, 2000

LEXMARK INTERNATIONAL, INC.   1992–2000
Senior Consultant, Education and Government Sales, 2000
Special Assistant to the Director, Healthcare Sales, 1999–2000
District Sales Manager, 1997–1999
Senior Program Manager, Strategic Alliances, 1996
Senior Account Executive, 1994–1996
Account Systems Engineer /National Account Executive, 1992–1993

INTERNATIONAL BUSINESS MACHINES CORPORATION   1987–1992
Account Systems Engineer, 1990–1992
Printing and Desktop Publishing Specialist, 1988–1990
Dealer Account Representative, 1987–1988

EDUCATION

Bachelor of Business Administration, Marketing, Magna cum Laude
University of Houston, Houston, Texas

Key Points for Chapter 6

"Success is biting off more than you can chew, and chewing it."
—Anonymous

Key Questions	Answers
What is the difference between each resume style? When should I choose a particular style?	The following chart explains the different types of competency-based resumes.

Resume Style	Most Effective When...	Style
Competency-Based Chronological	• Used for traditional organizations. • You want to work in the same field or industry. • There are no significant interruptions in work experience. • You have received no demotions. • Emphasis is on work history.	1. List accomplishments under each position. 2. Begin with your most current job and work your way back in time. 3. Summary and accomplishment statements are written with a competency-based focus.
Competency-Based Functional	• You have interruptions in your work history. • You have been demoted. • You have changed fields. • Emphasis is on accomplishments. • You are selling a service, such as consulting, to customers.	1. List accomplishments under each function. 2. Begin with the most important function for the position you are applying. 3. Summary and accomplishment statements are written with a competency-based focus. 4. Chronological lists of your employment history are listed after your accomplishments, near the end of the resume, but before education or other sections.
Direct Competency-Based	• Used for competency-based organizations either when applying for the first time or seeking promotions or transfers within the company. • You want to showcase your accomplishments in each competency area. • Emphasis is focused on clearly identified competency requirements.	1. List accomplishments under each competency. 2. Begin with the most important competency for the position you are applying. 3. Summary and accomplishment statements are written with a competency-based focus. 4. Chronological list if past positions are included at the end of the resume with most recent listed first.
Competency Based Electronic Resume	• You are sending a resume via e-mail. • You are posting your resume on a Website—or on a job search Website. • You are writing an ASCII resume requested by an employer.	1. Identify keywords. 2. Make sure to use key competencies in your keyword summary. 3. List key competencies early in the section. 4. The design can be a functional, chronological, or a direct competency-based resume.
Can I combine resume styles?	• Yes, but make sure your first step is to determine the key competencies needed by your target organization. • Depending on the employer's needs and how well your experience and background match the position, you may decide to use a combination of resume styles.	

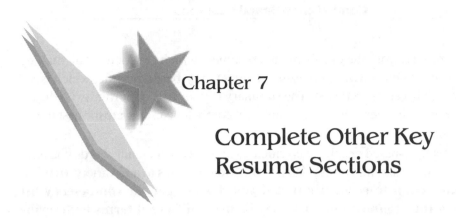

Chapter 7

Complete Other Key Resume Sections

In the last chapter we talked about the importance of providing evidence that you have the competencies needed to be successful on the job. But what else is important? How else do you sell yourself effectively?

When we read a good newspaper, we respond to more than just the facts in the articles. The newspaper editor also makes decisions about the right headlines, location of the article, word choice, format, photographs, editorial cartoons, and layout to be able to convince the readers that the newspaper is worth buying.

You need to convince the people reading your resume that *you* are worth buying. Even if the basic facts support your candidacy, you need to present your accomplishments and all the other information about you in a way that makes your professionalism clear to the decision-maker. Presentation matters. You need to sell yourself to the organization you want to work for by selling your competencies.

We talked about writing competency-based accomplishment statements in Chapter 5. In this chapter we're going to cover the other important sections of a resume, including the summary, education, technical skills, and other information sections. These sections, if written correctly, can provide additional evidence that you have the "right stuff"—the competencies employers need.

One of the keys to writing an effective resume is to be honest, but be sure to be diplomatically honest, not brutally honest. You want to emphasize the things that will help you be perceived in a positive way by the reader and de-emphasize the things that would hurt you.

Summary or Profile

This is one of the most important parts of any resume because if it is written well, it sells your background. The summary section has almost completely replaced the objective on the resume because it is a much more effective way to sell you to the person making the decision.

We have moved from the old-fashioned resumes, which are focused on making your resume about you and your goals, to a competency-based resume, which is focused on the employer's needs first. The summary is your first opportunity on the resume to show the employer that you have the right competencies and are the best match for the opportunity.

In a competency-based resume, it is critical to include competency words you have selected. Use synonyms and words related to the competencies to add variety. **In addition, it is important to recognize that if you did not get the competency list directly from the organization, they may be using different terms to describe the competency. For example, "Achieves Results" can easily be listed as "Achieves Goals."**

Almost every career coach has a different style of writing summaries. We'll show you several styles in the resume examples included in the book; you can see which ones you like the best.

One approach is to start out with the job title or what you would call yourself professionally. Then write about your expertise, job-related strengths, and your strengths in the competency areas. Include certifications such as CPA, and other skills such as being proficient in Spanish and English. Some experts like to separate out some of the strengths into bullets; some don't. Depending on what you think will be the most effective for the people who will read the resume, these bullets can be used for strengths and skills...**or to highlight your competencies**.

In general, the summary section of the resume should be between five and nine lines, unless you are using the bulleted style.

Technical Skills

This section, which is optional, is most important to include in resumes for technical professionals—particularly for most IT positions and for many engineers. Depending on how critical technical skills are for the position, it can be the second section on the resume (after the summary), or can be placed after the experience section on a chronological resume, or placed after the work history section in a functional resume. You would want to place it higher on the resume if it is more critical for the position.

For example, if a company is looking for a programmer, your relevant software skills are critical—probably the first thing the reader is going to be looking for. Make it easy for the reader to find this information on the resume by setting up a separate section.

Education

This section of the resume is probably the most common place for people to not tell the truth. We can all think of examples of people who lost their jobs, or at least were severely disciplined, for not telling the truth about their degrees.

In 2002 the athletic director for Dartmouth College resigned after his employer found out that he had not completed his master's degree. He had made the mistake of claiming that he had that degree on his resume.

The president of the United States Olympic Committee resigned after her employer discovered she had not received her bachelor's degree from Colorado State or her doctorate from the University of Arizona.

Unfortunately, this list is long. And it is important to understand that it is increasingly easy for employers to find out if you really do have your degree. You may be able to get away with not telling the truth in some situations for some period of time. But we strongly recommend that you do not falsify *any* information on your resume.

So what should you talk about on your resume in this section?

Start with your most recent degree and work backwards. These are the critical pieces to include:

* Name of college or university.

* Degree.

* Major(s), minors(s), concentration(s).

If your degree is 10 to 15 years old, use your judgment to determine whether the degree is going to be perceived as recent enough to help you. For example, the number of changes in the IT field in the last 15 years makes a 15-year-old computer science degree less current and marketable than degrees from other professional areas, such as accounting, where there have not been as many changes.

Think first about the competencies the employer is looking for, including functional competencies.

If you had three majors in your MBA program, make sure to list first the major that demonstrates competency in the most important area. For example, if you want to be hired as a human resources professional, list your majors this way: human resources, marketing, and finance. If you are trying for a finance job, list them in this order: finance, marketing, and human resources.

What you write first in any list is what people remember. Emphasize what counts the most by listing it first when you build your competency-based resume.

If you have recently graduated, you may need to include your GPA. Pick your strongest GPA (overall or in your major) and list it first. Consider leaving it off if it is below a 3.0.

Even if you spent your college years "developing your social skills," you may still be a good candidate for the right employer. By writing a competency-based resume, you are emphasizing why your competencies will help the employer be more successful.

Within a few years, you will have enough experience to write about so that your grades in college become less important.

If you don't have your degree yet, write about when you expect to complete the degree, such as "M.A. in Professional Writing expected June 2006." If you have taken some college courses, you will need to make a judgment call as to whether it will help you or not to write, "Completed 18 credit hours at University of Miami."

Other Information

What other information should you include on your resume?

Some experts believe that the best resumes contain no personal information. But it really comes down to a case-by-case approach; you have to make a decision about what information will really help your candidacy the most.

It wasn't that long ago that resumes typically included information about the candidate's height, weight, age, marital status, children, and their excellent health (everyone 30 years ago had excellent health, at least on their resumes!). And of course, references were always "available on request."

We don't include this kind of information today—and haven't for more than 20 years. Today's resumes are more focused on the things that directly relate to our ability to do the job. And we also are trying to use our space as productively as possible.

If you are going to include information about your background that is not related to your work experience or education, remember that the best information to include is the kind that provides evidence that you are strong in competency areas. For example, if you are interested in a public relations position, having strong writing skills is an extremely important competency. If you want to be the manager of community affairs, showing leadership in community activities is critical.

Be careful to remember that the experience needs to be relevant and appropriate for the position you are interested in being considered for. The 45 articles you've written would be an asset if you are looking for a position in research or at a university; that many articles may make someone in the corporate world perceive you as an academic and out of touch with his world. So use this kind of information when it will help you seem more competent for the position and the organization.

Don't include information that might cause someone to eliminate you as a candidate unless you absolutely have to. Remember that even hiring managers have biases and prejudices, so don't give them a reason on the resume to reject you. If you have been very active with political or religious groups that someone may perceive as being out of the mainstream, please don't volunteer that on your resume. And even being active in the most normal, mainstream groups may get you eliminated from consideration because the decision-maker's ex-wife or ex-husband may have been a part of the group.

Play it safe if you are going to include other information.

Choosing what to include in your resume can be challenging. Review your resume from the employer's perspective. Look at your skills, competencies, and other attributes from many angles. Ask how some of the things you have included may be misinterpreted or viewed in a negative way. If it is at all questionable, leave it out. Weigh the positives and negatives of each entry.

Remember, this is your opportunity to make that positive first impression, so use it wisely. When you are invited in for an interview, your resume is used as a reference for many of the questions you will be asked. Make sure your resume highlights how wonderful and talented you really are, and be ready to back up what you have presented.

Key Points for Chapter 7	
"Wise men talk because they have something to say; fools talk because they have to say something." —Plato	
Key Questions	**Answers**
Why are the other sections in my resume so important?	• While marketing your competencies you must remember you are also marketing your image and what is unique about your background and experiences. • A lot of applicants spend time polishing their accomplishment statements only to underestimate the importance of the rest of their resume. Presentation matters.
Why is the summary so important?	• It is the first part of your resume and the first impression you are making to the employer. • It highlights the best of what you have to offer. • It condenses your accomplishments and personality into one key section. • It compels the reviewer to read the rest of your resume.
How do I make my summary competency-based?	• It is critical to include words or synonyms in your summary from the competencies you have selected. Use words related to the competencies the employer needs to be successful.
Would you give me a general checklist to write a summary?	• Start out with the job title or what you would call yourself professionally. • Write about your expertise, job-related strengths, and your strengths in the competency areas. • Include certifications such as a CPA, and other skills such as being proficient in Spanish and English. • You might want to separate out your strengths, or competencies, into bulleted points for emphasis.
I am in a technical field. What can I do to enhance my resume?	• You can include a section right after the summary called "Technical Skills" or something similar. This is a good way to highlight relevant software, programs, or certifications that demonstrate competencies that your potential employer would be interested in.

Key Points for Chapter 7 (continued)	
Key Questions	**Answers**
I am in a technical field. What can I do to enhance my resume?	• You can include a section right after the summary called "Technical Skills" or something similar. This is a good way to highlight relevant software, programs, or certifications that demonstrate competencies and that your potential employer would be interested in.
What do I need to be concerned about with the Education section?	• Be careful when you include your degree, GPA, and graduation date (you don't always have to include the date) that you are accurate with your details. *It just may be checked by an employer you really want to work for!*
What are the rules for including my education?	• Start with your most recent degree and work backwards. • Include: Name of college or university and city, state, degree, major(s), minors(s), concentration(s). • If you've received the degree within the last 10 years, include the year you received the degree. When your degree is more than 11 to 15 years old, consider leaving the year off. • List the major first that demonstrates competency in the most important area. • If you don't have your degree yet, write about when you expect to complete the degree.

Chapter 8

Review, Revise, and Polish the Resume

Baseball legend Yogi Berra said, "It's déjà vu all over again."

When we are writing a resume, it sometimes seems like déjà vu because we spend so much time rewriting, editing, revising, and polishing our resume. And that's simply to get the resume developed for the first time you need it.

But then there's more déjà vu. Each time you've identified another position you're interested in, you should plan to spend even more time to make sure the resume has been refocused to consider the needs of the new employer or the new position. You may need to add more accomplishments, edit the ones you've already written, or choose to delete some.

It might help you to think of this process a little bit like developing a pearl. There's usually a relationship between the luster on the pearl and the price it goes for. So keep polishing!

The great news is that if you've written a strong competency-based resume, you should feel pretty good about your accomplishments and how the resume looks. You'll get to have that same "feel good" sense more than once! You're probably going to feel quite competent too!

Review the Resume

When you've finished the first draft of the resume, take the time to read it carefully to make sure it says what you want it to say.

First read it for content and then read it for correctness. Here are the steps to follow to make sure your resume is as complete and polished as possible after you have completed your first draft.

1. Read your summary and accomplishment statements again to make sure that you've included the information that does the best job of showing that you are as strong as possible in the competencies the employer cares the most about.

2. Ask your mentor and former managers and coworkers you trust to review the resume and let you know if they think of some significant accomplishments that you may have left out. Also ask for their help in identifying accomplishments where you've undersold or oversold your background so that you can rewrite the statement so that it will work more effectively for you. It is always important to thank them for their help—in person, in writing, or in an e-mail. This will also help you with keeping your own network happy and willing to work with you in the future.

    Remember that your reviewer should be giving you suggestions about content, not resume style, writing, or grammar. Recognize the strengths of the individual, and be careful about having someone outside the career consulting or human resources fields rewrite your resume. Even within these fields, people have different levels of skill when they are writing resumes.

    One private client came in to see us with one of the worst resumes we've seen after her good friend, a paralegal, reviewed her resume and decided to rewrite it. The original resume, while not perfect, was far better than the one the paralegal wrote.

3. Make sure you have not included anything that will cause an employer to "screen you out" if you can help it. Please review Chapter 5 to give you the details about the type of statements that could cause you to be screened out.

4. Check the tone and the language to ensure you are saying things in a positive way. You may also want to look at the company's Website and any written publications to get a sense of the writing style typically used in the company, and see if the style, tone, and terminology you've used in the resume is compatible. Pay particular attention to the language the company has used for describing competencies.

5. Never send your resume to anyone without putting it through spell-check. But spell-check won't catch grammatical mistakes, just the words that are misspelled. You still need to know basic usage, grammar, and punctuation rules.

    One school newspaper did a review of a movie where the reviewer admitted he needed some moral support because of the violence in the film. The reviewer wrote that he brought his family and *fiends* with him to the movie. Remember that a *friend* becomes a *fiend* if one letter is left out of the word.

    We suggest that you ask one of your smarter fiends to help you review the resume for mechanical mistakes. (Did you catch that?)

6. Check for consistency. Make sure that you've ended every accomplishment statement with a period—or without one. Our recommendation is

to use the periods at the end of the statements, but this recommendation is simply a preference.

Remembering to be consistent with commas before the word "and" when you are including a list is another problem area for many people. We know that the current preference is to include the comma; we can also remember being taught by our English teachers not to include the comma.

In both examples the key is to be consistent with the way you do it.

7. Review the resume for overused words and phrases. Variety in language helps keep the reader's interest—we get bored reading a resume where every accomplishment statement starts with the same word such as "managed" or "saved."

8. Check to make sure that every accomplishment statement starts with a powerful action verb. Review Chapter 5 to ensure you've followed the recommendations on how to write accomplishment statements.

Revise and Polish the Resume

Once you've reviewed the resume, received feedback on it from other competent professionals, and identified the words and phrases you need to change, it is time to edit, revise the resume, and rewrite some or all of it.

When you've finally made the changes, if you do not have an interview in the afternoon and can wait to finish the resume for a day or two, put the resume in a file and review it again when you've taken a break of at least several hours.

It may help to think of your resume as a work in progress—you can always make some changes later. Your resume should be evolving and improving as you:

★ Receive feedback during the job search.

★ Develop new competencies and skills.

★ Earn recognition, honors, or degrees.

★ Apply for new positions and new assignments.

★ Recognize that the traditional approaches are not effective for your situation.

Pay Attention to How the Resume Looks

Here are some basic tips to make your resume look as sharp as possible.

Font: Use Times New Roman or a similar looking font. High-tech companies often use Arial and Helvetica. Stick with one font throughout the resume. The goal is for the resume to look as business-like and professional as possible. Keep the font size between 10 and 12 points, depending upon how your information fits on the pages. Be careful about how often you use boldface, italics, or underlining.

Margins: In general, we prefer to leave top, bottom, right, and left margins at least 0.8 inches to ensure that there is enough white space to keep the reader from feeling overwhelmed by the business of the material on the resume.

 Hint: Hold the resume far enough away from you that you can't read the individual words. You want the resume to be easy to read and pleasing to the eye. Does it have enough white space (areas where there is no writing)? Are the pages and margins balanced?

You can use font size and margins to make sure that the break between the first and second page falls in a logical place or to balance the look of the page. It is important to remember to put your name and the page number at the top of the second page (shown in the two-page resume examples) to ensure that if the two pages become separated, they can easily be put back together.

Prepare for the Future

Once your resume has been reviewed, edited, and revised for a particular opportunity, we recommend that you set up a system to keep track of your own competencies and accomplishments. We think of this system as a competency-based filing system.

The system can be set up using a spreadsheet program or a database. By using these programs you will have the flexibility to sort based upon competencies, accomplishments, position, or the date that something happened. When you have loaded the information from your resume into the program, it is important to keep it updated. Remember to go into your filing system at least once each month and write accomplishment statements describing what you have achieved, and which competencies you've developed.

You should be keeping track of your own competencies each month by asking yourself:

★ Which of the key competencies for my position have I strengthened or developed this month?

★ What accomplishments did I have during this period that provide evidence that I am competent in the areas my organization cares about?

★ What accomplishments did I have that show that I'm competent in other areas listed as competencies in this book?

Develop well-written accomplishment statements and include the new information in your database, spreadsheet, or filing system. Then you're more prepared to update your resume the next time you want to apply for a new position.

 Hint: Having this information ready also puts you in a situation where you can easily impress your current manager with how well prepared you are before your next performance appraisal. If you are currently working for an organization that uses competency-based performance appraisals, a few weeks before your appraisal, provide your manager with a list of the relevant competencies and what your most impressive accomplishments are under each competency heading. It will help you look like a star.

Key Points for Chapter 8

"I try to do the right thing at the right time. They may just be little things, but usually they make the difference between winning and losing."

—Kareem Abdul-Jabbar

Key Questions	Answers
What is the process for my first resume edit?	First read it for content and then read it for correctness.
What are some editing hints for reviewing my resume?	• Ask your mentor, friends, and past managers to review it and offer feedback. • Look at it with fresh eyes. Take a break from reading your resume and look at it the next day. • Use your spell-check but don't rely on it for every edit. Check every word before sending it on. Reading the document backwards helps you check each word for accuracy. • Check for tone and language first, then check for grammar, next punctuation, next for misspellings and wrong word usage, next for consistency, and last for visual appeal.
Why should my resume be considered a work-in-progress?	Your resume should be evolving and improving as you: 1. Receive feedback during the job search. 2. Develop new competencies and skills. 3. Earn recognition, honors, or degrees. 4. Apply for new positions and new assignments. 5. Recognize that the traditional approaches are not effective for your situation.

Key Points for Chapter 8 (continued)	
Key Questions	**Answers**
Should I keep track of my accomplishments?	Yes, set up a system to keep track of your own competencies and accomplishments. We think of this system as a competency-based filing system. You should be keeping track of your own competencies each month by asking yourself: 1. Which of the key competencies have I strengthened or developed this month? 2. What new accomplishments provide evidence that I am competent in the areas my organization cares about? 3. What accomplishments have I completed that show that I am also competent in other areas?
Is this competency-based filing system used for any other purpose?	Yes, it is an excellent marketing tool for you. Create a competency-based accomplishment sheet to present to your employer when you want to be considered for a new position and before your performance appraisal. *Remember to give your manager your competency-based accomplishment list a few weeks before your evaluation so he or she can consider it when writing the final written performance review.*

Chapter 9

Check to Make Sure Your Resume Is Complete

At this point you have carefully read each of the chapters on writing a competency-based resume, and you understand the benefits of completing a polished, targeted resume. We thought a quick reference checklist would be helpful for you. All successful treasure hunters rely on a step-by-step detailed map to find that cache of hidden gold, so here is your treasure map to completing your competency-based resume. The job search is an adventure, so don't miss any of the steps on your map. If you follow these steps like Indiana Jones, the prize will be yours.

Competency-Based Resume Writing Checklist

The most important consideration when writing competency-based resumes is to keep the focus on the employer's competency requirements.

Step	Activity		Key Focus Questions and Tasks	Reference Pages	Complete
1.	Gathering Information		*Compile a checklist for each target position.*		
		a.	What is your target position?	—	
			Task: List specific positions and titles.	51	
		b.	What organization do I want to work for?	—	
			Task: List your target companies and organizations.	51	
2.	Compiling Competency List		*Identify relevant competencies.*	25–30	
		a.	What are the competencies required for the target position?	—	
			Task: List competencies required by the target organization/company. Check advertisements, job postings, performance reviews, and company Website/handbook for a competency list; ask networking contacts. *Make sure you use the same terminology as the target company.*	26–29	
		b.	If the competencies aren't directly identified, ask: 1. Are the competencies identified in the resources listed in Appendix A but not called competencies? Look under "Requirements," "Dimensions," or "Qualifications." Read closely to see if typical competencies are included in the ads, etc.	149–160	

Step	Activity	Key Focus Questions and Tasks	Reference Pages	Complete
		2. What are the most common competencies used by competitors in the same industry?	149–160	
		3. What are the competencies listed online at employment Websites such as Monster.com for my professional area?		
		4. Which competencies listed in Chapter 3 are the most relevant to the position I'm interested in?		
		Task: Review organization resources to look for "indirect" competencies. Research similar companies and industries and identify competencies (or additional competencies) for the position you are seeking. Look at online employment sites to see if competencies are listed for comparable positions. Review the list of competencies included in Chapter 3 and choose 10 to 15 of the most relevant for your position.	27–29	
	c.	Which are the *best* competencies to use? Which competencies are the most critical to be successful in the position?	—	
		Task: Compile a final list of competencies to use in your job search.	25–30	
	d.	Ask yourself, "What are my strongest competencies?"	—	
		Task: List your strongest competencies. Look at the list of most **standard competencies used by organizations** listed in Chapter 3. List all of your competencies. Some may be different than the list of target competencies identified in Appendix A.	25–30	
		Task: Identify your competencies that match those listed for the target position. These are the competencies you want to highlight in your resume—in the summary and in your accomplishment statements.	25–30 35–42	

Step	Activity		Key Focus Questions and Tasks	Reference Pages	Complete
3.	**Write Resume Summary**	a.	What are the most important competencies to be successful in the position?	—	
			Task: Write a summary clearly identifying how you are strong in the competency areas identified. Keep the sentences short, easy to review, and precise. Include what you do best, what you are known for, and special skills related to the relevant competencies, such as language, degrees, and education.	75–76	
			Task: Review your summary for energy, tone, terminology, and especially the image you are projecting. *Remember that readers will have their first impression of you based on the summary section of your resume.*	81–83	
		b.	What are my accomplishments that best meet the competency requirements for this individual position?	—	
			Task: Write accomplishments for each competency that you can. Start with your current position and work your way through your work history, going by job titles.	54–60	
			Task: Write accomplishment statements addressing the situation or problem, action, and results, sometimes called P-A-R. Always use an action verb at the beginning of your statements.	55–56	
			Task: Prioritize accomplishment statements in order of importance within each competency or job title.	60	

Step	Activity		Key Focus Questions and Tasks	Reference Pages	Complete
		c.	What competency-based resume style—functional, chronological, direct competency, or combination—will promote my background the most effectively to the decision-makers?	63–73	
			Task: Arrange competency-based accomplishment statements in priority order for the style selected.	73	
4.	**Write the Rest of Your Resume**		*Be succinct, focused, and honest.*		
		a.	What degrees, licenses, or certifications have I earned that demonstrate experience in a competency area or in another way meet the needs of the target position?	—	
			Task: List your educational accomplishments. Start with your most recent degree and work backwards. These are the critical pieces to include:　Name of college or university.　Degree.　Major(s), minors(s), concentration(s).　If you've received the degree within the last 10 years, include the year; when your degree is more than 15 years old, leave it off—unless there is a good reason to include it.	76–78	
			Task: List all licenses and certifications. It may help you demonstrate competencies or skills more clearly if you allocate a section in your resume to specific technical skills. This can be listed after the summary if the skills are particularly critical for the position or before or after the education section if they are less important.	78–79	

Step	Activity		Key Focus Questions and Tasks	Reference Pages	Complete
		b.	What activities or volunteer work have I done that provide evidence of experience in a competency area?	—	
			Task: List activities, hobbies, and volunteer positions. Carefully assess the potential benefit of every inclusion; only include it if you are confident it will be perceived positively. Most people do not include activities, volunteer work, or hobbies on their resumes. Under any circumstance, avoid including hobbies and volunteer projects that may be seen as controversial.	78–79	
5.	**Edit Resume**	a.	Have I used certain words too often?	—	
			Task: Review the resume for overused words. *Please note that in a checklist we can choose to overuse words such as "review"! With a resume, you need to be more careful!*	83	
		b.	Is the resume written clearly? Did I achieve my main purpose in writing this resume? Am I getting across how strong a candidate I am for this position? Is it easy to see that I have good experience in the relevant competency areas?	—	
			Task: Review the resume for grammar and spelling. Use spell-check on the resume.	82	
			Task: Review the resume for punctuation. Make a decision to end all sentences with periods or leave them off. Most importantly, be consistent.	82–83	
			Task: Reread the resume to ensure that everything is written in the past tense—except accomplishments that are ongoing or happening now.	81–83	

Step	Activity	Key Focus Questions and Tasks	Reference Pages	Complete
		Task: Review the language in the summary section and in accomplishment statements. Remember shorter phrases are usually more powerful than longer ones. Eliminate unnecessary words that don't add anything to the content (a, an, numerous, various, that).	81–83	
		Task: Review the resume for tone. Does it match the tone and style in the organization's Website and other company publications? *Take the time to go to the Website and review the language and tone the organization uses to describe itself. Look through other organization publications.*	81–83	
6.	**Review Resume for Visual Appeal**	a. What is the first impression my resume projects? Does it have image and visual appeal?	—	
		Task: Look for balanced white space (without any text). White space allows the eyes to rest and is more appealing for the reader.	84	
		Task: If it is a two-page resume, make sure page breaks come at a logical place (that is, between sections). Make the second page of your resume fill at least two-thirds of the page by working with your font size and using spacing or page breaks. Watch out for unnatural page breaks between paragraphs, accomplishment statements, or job descriptions.	84	

Step	Activity	Key Focus Questions and Tasks	Reference Pages	Complete
		Task: Remember to include your name and the page number at the top of the second page of your resume. *This will help if the hard copy pages of the resume get separated. Your name is already at the top of the first page!*	84	
		Task: Adjust the margins and font size to balance your resume on both pages. (The font should be between 10 and 12 picas.)	84	
		Task: Use one font unless there is a compelling reason to use a second one. The most common font used in resumes today is Times New Roman. Sans serif fonts, such as Ariel, tend to be used in technology areas.	83	
		Task: Make sure to use underlining, all caps, italics, and bold carefully and rarely.	83	

Chapter 10

Look at Case Studies for Ideas to Make the Resume Stronger

By three methods we may learn wisdom: First, by reflection, which is noblest; second, by imitation, which is easiest; and third, by experience, which is the bitterest.

—Confucius

Even though we are showing you a new way to write resumes in this book, we are going to encourage you to pay attention to Confucius. Particularly the second part of the quote.

We're not against reflection or experience, but we recommend that you read through Chapters 10 and 11 looking for ideas that you can imitate or adapt to make your resume stronger. Will you learn wisdom? We're not sure about that, but we can definitely tell you that it is easier to modify than it is to create the resume from the beginning.

In this chapter we've provided you with some case studies to give you an opportunity to see how we addressed some *sticky* issues when we developed competency-based resumes for four individuals. Many of us have some things in our background or work history that might be difficult to explain in a resume. By looking at the four cases we've included, you will see examples of how we decided to address some issues or situations that make the individual's issues, or weak areas, less obvious.

Because a competency-based resume focuses on two things—the employer's needs first and your matching competencies second—it will always work more effectively for you, but particularly when you have some sticky issues that make your work history look less stellar.

We believe you are a star. You need to believe it too. And your resume needs to reflect how strong you really are, and to de-emphasize the problems in your work history as much as possible.

You can do this. We'll show you what the issues were for four candidates and what solutions we developed.

Meet Jeff Oldham, a sales professional; Mary Ann Stevens, a human resources vice president; Roger Cassell, a purchasing agent; and Sarah Whitehead, a recent graduate. Two of them had been unemployed for a long period of time when we met them. One was getting ready to lose a job because her company had been acquired by a competitor. And the last one was graduating and looking for her first employer.

All of them were great people with good potential. Each of them had something in their work history or professional background that could cause an employer to reject them—if their resume did not present them as positively as possible. You might have some of these same issues.

Case Study: Sales Professional
Situation

Jeff Oldham had been unemployed for 20 months when his sister suggested that he get some additional help in his job search—that something wasn't working right or he would have found some work by that point in time. He had worked in sales and sales management for two major high-tech and peripherals companies before losing his last job during a layoff. By the time we met him, he was discouraged and in financial trouble.

When we started working with him, Jeff had a difficult time explaining the kind of work he wanted to do. Even though he had been successful in sales and had won a number of sales awards from his companies, he was frustrated with selling and told us that he was ready to do something else. He had taken a number of career tests and talked about wanting his work to help him be self-actualized. The resume he was using was several pages long, confusing to read, and didn't clearly point to any professional area.

Resume Issues and Concerns

1. He had been unemployed for 20 months.

2. He was not able to explain what he wanted to do next.

3. Until we reached a decision about what types of positions to target, we could not complete a competency-based resume for him. **Remember that one of the key steps in writing a competency-based resume is to *always* think first about the employer's needs.**

Action

After a session or two of career coaching, we talked about his comment about self-actualization and agreed that his main objective at this point should be to get a job now and continue to work toward self-actualization later. Because he had worked and succeeded at sales before, the fastest way for him to get a new position would be to focus on looking at opportunities in sales that would also use his ability to pick up technical information quickly.

We recommended writing a competency-based resume to help focus the resume on his competencies and accomplishments. Because he had been unemployed for such a long period of time, we thought it made more sense for him to avoid using his competency-based chronological resume, which emphasizes his recent unemployment as the first thing in the "Experience" or "Work History" sections of his resume. Even though there are ways of de-emphasizing a period of little work, such as using the terms "consultant" or "independent contractor," we recommended using the two other major competency-based resume types, because it would give him the opportunity to show his competencies and accomplishments *before* providing his work history.

When we first worked with Jeff on his resume, we asked him to help identify the *right* competencies for a sales position in a technical area. We agreed that being considered a high performer in the sales area usually meant someone who sold the most products or services, or someone who "brought in" the highest revenue. In other words, the best performers in sales always are achievers—they achieve their results.

We also looked online to develop a list of competencies for technical sales professionals. In the online advertisement for a sales professional at StorageTek (discussed on pages 52–54), the list of competencies also includes:

1. Customer Focus.
2. Interpersonal Savvy.
3. Technical Learning.
4. Perseverance.
5. Business Acumen.
6. Dealing With Ambiguity.
7. Presentation Skills.
8. Organizing.
9. Negotiating.

After reviewing the list, Jeff decided that he would focus on developing accomplishment statements around "Achieving Results," "Customer Focus," "Interpersonal Savvy," and "Organizing" for his competency-based resumes. Because "Achieving Results" is usually considered the most important by the hiring managers—and he'd certainly achieved results in the past—we listed that first on his competency-based direct resume.

Please notice when you look at Jeff's resumes that we managed to include most of the other key competencies for this position in the summary section and as part of certain accomplishment statements.

Competency-Based Combination Resume

JEFFREY K. OLDHAM
5011 Red Bridge Drive
Houston, TX 77087
(281) 858-0130
jkoldham2@swbell.net

SUMMARY

District Sales Manager with expertise in business development, solution sales, and technology. Significant experience in new product marketing: product launch and marketing strategy, strategic alliance building, project management, and consultative selling. Skilled at relationship building, channel and OEM sales, contract negotiations, and closing sales. Consistent top performer with record of achieving results, generating revenue, exceeding sales quotas, and delivering exceptional customer service. Excellent interpersonal, organizational, presentation, and writing skills.

WORK HISTORY

CONSULTANT   **2002–2003**

ECG CORPORATION   **2000–2001**
Director, Business Development, 2000–2001
Senior Program Manager, 2000
Results/Customer Service
- Proposed first company-wide print and document strategy with expected savings of $20 million per year.
- Developed sales/marketing campaign awarded national quality award based on Six Sigma criteria.

Interpersonal Skills/Organizational Awareness
- Worked with key departments to define technology needs and product development courses, market positioning, network deployment, and partner activities.
- Developed marketing strategy for "sell through" and "sell with" activities between company and preferred technology vendor.

LEXMARK INTERNATIONAL, INC.   **1992–2000**
Senior Consultant, Education and Government Sales, 2000
Special Assistant to Director, Healthcare Sales, 1999–2000
Results
- Selected for Winner's Circle for top 2% of U.S. sales professionals.
- Named Account Executive of the Year, three years, and of the Quarter, 14 quarters.
- Sold one million custom-built inkjet printers after identifying partnership opportunity with Micron.

Impact and Influence
- Managed major client business engagements across U.S. to maximize healthcare team revenue; exceeded $6 million revenue goal in five months.

JEFFREY K. OLDHAM **Page 2**

WORK HISTORY (Continued)

LEXMARK INTERNATIONAL, INC.
District Sales Manager, 1997–1999
Senior Program Manager, Strategic Alliances, 1996
Senior Account Executive, 1994–1996
Account Systems Engineer/National Account Executive, 1992–1993
Results
- Achieved highest revenues of first-year sales managers and ranked in top 10% of all sales managers in employee satisfaction ratings, 1998.
- Managed team responsible for $12 million national purchase agreement with Columbia/HCA.
- Won Sales Director Award as top-ranked sales performer in U.S. Healthcare division, two consecutive years.
- Coached sales and technical support team to develop more innovative sales strategies; increased sales 20% annually per territory.
- Grew revenues in new healthcare territory to $2.6 million in two years.

Impact and Influence / Interpersonal
- Facilitated team of 12 employees to develop "Business Advisor," CD-based consulting tool for U.S. sales force; exceeded functionality and stayed under budget.
- Mentored 11 new hires on sales team; developed, implemented, and tracked results of marketing and sales strategies for team.
- Worked as key member of team developing marketing campaign and presentations to introduce *total cost of printing* concept to customers.

Customer Service / Organizational Awareness
- Coordinated team introducing first global 24 by 7 non-stop service and parts delivery offering for NCR.
- Managed CRM project for Global Strategic Sourcing, with projected customer satisfaction rating improving from 67% to 95%.
- Convinced clinical and IT managers to purchase platform upgrades despite competition from onsite vendor; managed rollout at County Hospital District.
- Recognized for successfully managing 11 sales/technical/administrative employees selling printing equipment/services to healthcare customers in 23 state region.

IBM CORPORATION 1987–1992
Account Systems Engineer, 1990–1992
Printing and Desktop Publishing Specialist, 1988–1990
Dealer Account Representative, National Distribution Division, 1987–1988
- Selected for IBM 100% Club.
- Improved IBM printer market share in territory from 9% to 20% in two years.

EDUCATION

Bachelor of Business Administration, Marketing, Magna cum Laude
University of Houston, Houston, Texas

Result

In addition to the comptency-based combination resume shown, Jeff's other resumes are included in Chapter 6 on pages 67–72. He worked primarily with the competency-based functional resume and the competency-based direct resume, and used the Internet as his primary source of job opportunities. Even though he knew networking is still the number one way most people find jobs, he felt that after 20 months of looking for a job, he had already called most of the people that were easy for him to contact in his primary network. We identified ways for him to continue networking the competency-based way, and he did the things we suggested, but he relied more heavily on jobsites as he began his job search with the new resumes.

Within two days of posting his resume on Monster.com, CareerBuilder.com, and a few other jobsites, Jeff began to get calls. Within one week, he was getting interviews. Within three weeks, he was talking seriously to two large high-tech companies about positions as a sales representative and to one large communications company about working in a position where he would be managing a sales territory for them. Three weeks—three good opportunities.

Two weeks later, he had two job offers and a difficult decision to make.

Case Study: Human Resources Vice President
Situation

Mary Ann Stevens worked as vice president of human resources for a division of a Fortune 500 company that had recently announced the division was being sold to a competitor. She had been asked to stay during the transition period but had been told it was unlikely that the acquiring company would need another human resources executive at her level. She had worked for the division for nine years and before that, at the organization headquarters for 12 years. Since she left teaching and started to work in human resources, she had been with the same company, in progressively more responsible positions. She'd done well and had been recognized for her hard work.

In addition to what she had directly been told, Mary Ann was astute enough politically to decide that she did not fit the new company's culture (or style) and that even if they offered her a position, she should know what her options were. The best thing she could do now was to get ready for her next opportunity.

Resume Issues and Concerns

1. She had spent her entire career at the same company.

2. Her corporation had been in the news for financial misdeeds fairly recently along with Tyco, Martha Stewart, and Enron.

3. She was well past 40 and concerned that her age would work against her in the job search.

4. She had held the vice president title for nine years and thought that employers might not consider her for a job with equal responsibility and salary, but that had a less impressive director or manager title.

5. Because she was just beginning to think about her options, she had not identified a specific position she was interested in—or a company she wanted to work for. This meant that identifying the right competencies for her to emphasize on her resume would be challenging.

Action

We recommended writing two resumes for her—a competency-based functional resume and a competency-based direct resume.

It was clear that a traditional chronological resume wouldn't work as well for her because it would focus more on her work history and less on her accomplishments. We considered working with her to develop a competency-based chronological resume, but still felt that even though it would be a better choice because competencies are clearly included, it had some of the same drawbacks as a traditional chronological resume.

Even though she had been quite successful in her career, her longevity with the company could work against her if a hiring manager had concerns about her ability to adapt to the new organization and leave the old ways of doing things behind. **She would need to be prepared to demonstrate flexibility and adaptability during future interviews to convince managers with this bias that she would indeed be successful making the transition.**

Both types of chronological resumes wouldn't work as well for her because of her company's questionable reputation, which would be more prominently shown early in the resume. Her title would also be shown in the first part of the section on her experience, instead of the emphasis being on what she had accomplished.

*(Note: In some cases, people decide to use a title that is more recognized outside their organizations for their professional area. So if a vice president for a smaller organization is actually at the same level as a director or manager in a larger organization, many people choose to stay away from the vice president title on their resumes, if they think it might work against them. **The key here is to think about the organization's needs first.**)*

By using a competency-based functional resume or the direct resume style, her work history—including her well-known employer, her executive title, and the length of time she had spent with the employer—does not get as much emphasis as her competencies and her accomplishments.

Remember that by emphasizing the competencies the individual employer is looking for, you improve your chance of getting an interview. In this case, because she was just starting her job search, she did not have a specific list of competencies from one employer to look at when developing her competency-based accomplishment statements and the summary section for her resume.

We looked at the competency list included in Chapter 3, went online and looked at the competencies listed for human resources positions that day, and talked about what it took to be successful in a senior-level human resources position. After brainstorming a list of competencies, I asked her to pick 10 of the competencies that she thought were the most important to the hiring managers. The next step was to choose five or six of the competencies from this list that she knew were her own strengths, and emphasize those on her resumes. These are the competencies she chose as first, being the most important to organizations, and second, being ones in which she knew she had performed at a high level:

★ Organizational Awareness.

★ Strategic Orientation.

★ Impact and Influence.

★ Performance and Results Management.

★ Initiative.

★ Analytical Thinking.

We then went through each competency and developed accomplishment statements to demonstrate her expertise in each area. We asked behavioral questions to help her think about her accomplishments: *"Tell me about a time when you demonstrated initiative and it worked to benefit your organization."*

Once we looked at her list of examples, we worked with her to turn them into high-quality competency-based accomplishment statements. That session also helped us decide how to focus her summary section in a way that would work the most effectively to promote her background.

She understood that when she was applying for specific positions in the future, she would need to go back and rewrite parts of her resume to demonstrate the competencies that specific organization was looking for.

Result

After going through all the steps that we recommend to develop an effective competency-based resume, we wrote and revised Mary Ann's functional resume, which is shown on page 103. It should be easy for a sophisticated recruiter representing an organization looking for a senior-level human resources manager to tell from looking at her comptency-based functional resume that Mary Ann has the competencies the client is looking for.

Competency-Based Functional Resume

MARY ANN STEVENS

1723 Prairie Grove   214.870.1148
Dallas, TX 78077   mastevens@hotmail.com

SUMMARY

Human Resources Manager with expertise advising senior management on proactive human resources strategies and programs. Proven track record of developing business partnerships, facilitating performance initiatives, and coaching managers and employees to succeed with integrity. Certified Compensation Professional (CCP). Recognized for consistently achieving results and strengths in:

- Organizational Awareness
- Strategic Orientation
- Impact and Influence
- Performance Results Management
- Demonstrating Initiative
- Analytical Thinking

ACCOMPLISHMENTS

Human Resources Management
- Took initiative to provide oversight and advice to seven local human resources managers based in Venezuela, Argentina, United Kingdom, France, Jamaica, and Puerto Rico working with 4,000 employees; ensured alignment with corporate human resources strategies and practices.
- Recognized for building effective corporate culture after transportation company with 500 employees was acquired by identifying best practices from both companies.
- Managed team selecting and overseeing implementation of Ceridian integrated payroll/human resources system in 2000; reduced payroll cycle five days per month.
- Worked as key member of management team deciding to emphasize new name of subsidiary instead of name of parent company; managed team developing new brand and brand implementation in 90-day period.
- Represented human resources and investor relations during restructuring process; worked closely with outside lawyers to ensure compliance with bankruptcy process and correct handling of communications with employees and other stakeholders.

Training and Development
- Created individual development plans for seven supervisors and 18 employees in human resources department; discussed plans with each employee and mentored through year.
- Improved performance behavior for 1,200-employee company by developing five employee performance management/development processes to meet needs of different employee groups.
- Coached managers and employees including ex-military officer after he became Vice President of Operations; recognized by president of division after vice president developed participative management style, collaborative skills, and organizational sensitivities.

Mary Ann Stevens   **Page 2**

ACCOMPLISHMENTS (Continued)

Compensation and Benefits
- Designed and developed cash and equity incentive program in 2003 for 75 executives, managers, and key employees; provided more competitive compensation and ensured compliance with accounting board standards and changes.
- Worked closely with attorney to design 401(k) plan tied to profitability of company; provided more competitive benefits and improved ability to hire/retain employees.
- Managed team streamlining process for annual compensation reviews; saved four days of employee time after eliminating required approvals from department managers.

Employment
- Managed reorganization of field operations in 2002, combining four regions into three, downsized company 10% through severance and early retirement; completed reorganization in 30 days.
- Served on management team during acquisition of 500-employee division of Fortune 500 company; reduced staff of combined companies 50%.
- Developed first division-specific college recruiting program; trained recruiters and managed hiring of 25 engineers, accountants, and financial professionals in first year.

EMPLOYMENT HISTORY

CMG ENERGY, Dallas, TX   **1993–2004**
Vice President, Human Resources and Administration

CENTER STAR FUELS COMPANY, HOUSTON, TX AND OMAHA, NB   **1980–1992**
Vice President, Human Resources and Administration, 1987–1992
Director, Human Resources and Safety, 1986–1987
Manager, Personnel Resources, 1983–1986
Personnel Resources Administrator, 1982–1983
Compensation and Benefits Specialist, 1980–1982

EDUCATION

Master of Business Administration
University of Nebraska, Lincoln, NB

Bachelor of Arts, English
Educational Media Minor
University of Kansas, Lawrence, KS

Case Study: Purchasing Agent

Situation

Roger Cassell had lost his last full-time, regular position as a purchasing agent for a financial firm in early 2003. Although he had been able to get some contract work for two months, he had been unsuccessful in finding a regular job in his professional area when a friend suggested that he should meet with us.

Roger, like Jeff Oldham, was frustrated and concerned about what would happen to him. Unlike many of the people in the other case studies we've included in the chapter, Roger told us that he was a serious artist and worked in purchasing to provide the income so he could work on his art without having to worry about money. From an art perspective, he was doing well—his work was represented in several shows locally and throughout the northeastern United States. Because he was doing relatively well with his art, his confidence wasn't as shaken as it could have been.

Financially, he did not make enough from his art to cover many of his expenses. And the art took time from his job search. He needed to work, and he needed to work soon.

Resume Issues and Concerns

1. He had been unemployed for 12 months.

2. He was not sure whether to include information about his work as an artist on the resume.

3. He was convinced that he had to write a one-page resume.

4. He was not getting very many interviews.

5. Organizations use different titles to describe what Roger does for a living, including purchasing agent, buyer, and supply-chain representative.

Action

After talking with Roger, we told him that we thought the resume was his biggest problem. If you aren't getting many interviews, your resume is probably not selling your background effectively.

Once we looked at his resume, we could see why it wasn't working for him. It didn't give any specifics about what he had accomplished, and the reader could not tell anything about Roger's competencies.

Even though many career consultants still believe in one-page resumes, we think that one page is too limiting for people with substantial experience and **does not give you the space you need to demonstrate your competencies that the employer is looking for.** In Roger's case, we convinced him to develop a two-page resume (which is standard for most professionals or managers with 10 years or more of experience).

We then began looking at advertisements on career Websites for competencies for purchasing agents and buyers. We also looked at the list included in Chapter 3 of the most commonly used competencies. After reviewing the lists, Roger identified the six competencies he thought would be the most important to the people making the decision to interview him. Next, he identified which competencies on that list were also competencies he felt were strengths of his. He decided to focus on:

★ Achieving Results.

★ Initiative.

★ Identifying Solutions to Problems.

★ Customer Orientation.

After that, we talked about competency-based accomplishments, and he read through an early draft of Chapter 5 for this book. We worked with him on developing three accomplishment statements. He had demonstrated to us in this process that he had strong writing skills, so we encouraged him to do the first draft of the rest of the accomplishment statements focusing on demonstrating strengths in each key competency area.

After looking at the ads, he also decided to use the title "Purchasing Agent," on his resume.

Writing a competency-based resume helped focus the resume on his competencies and accomplishments. Because he had been unemployed for such a long period of time, we thought it made more sense for him to avoid using a competency-based chronological resume. We recommended using the two other major competency-based resume types: direct competency and competency-based functional.

Result

We were working with this client on his resume as we finished the final draft of this book. His original resume is included on page 107, and the revised, competency-based functional resume is on pages 108 to 109. The competency-based functional resume is very closely related to the direct competency resume, which would be achieved by changing the "Cost Savings" title to "Achieved Results," and the "Negotiations" title to "Influencing, Interpersonal Skills and Negotiations."

From talking with Roger, we knew that we'd be working with him to encourage him to do more networking. But even before having that conversation, he was starting to see results from his new resume. Within one week of getting his competency-based resume, Roger had been contacted for two interviews.

Original Resume

Roger T. Cassell
3051 Mayapple Rd., Stamford, CT 06903
203.529.0198 – rtcassell@aol.com

OBJECTIVE

To develop a purchasing and procurement career offering challenges, accountability, and opportunities for professional development and growth. My strengths include the ability to manage and resolve problems, negotiate contracts and proposals, research and organize special projects, all while maintaining innovation and adaptability.

PROFESSIONAL EXPERIENCE

9/02–2/03   **IBM – New York, NY**
Procurement Coordinator
Responsible for requisitions and purchase orders in SAP and Oracle for office supplies, books/subscriptions, and capital equipment. Customer service and problem resolution.

1991–2002   **MERRILL LYNCH – New York, NY**
Purchasing Group Leader
Supervision and training of staff as purchasing agent and assistant. Negotiated three-state, company-wide purchase of fax machines. Implementation of online ordering for printing and office supplies. Developed Rolodex order database.

1994–1997   **Purchasing Agent**
Creation of Merrill Lynch's first organized purchasing system. Initiated RFP/bidding process for contracted purchases. Consolidated office supply ordering system and initiated desktop delivery. Organized department order representatives.

1992–1994   **Receiving Clerk**
Created receiving clerk position as part-time and summer employee. Implemented computerized package receiving and tracking system. Implemented PC-based ordering system. Initiated first formal office supply bid.

EDUCATION

B.S. in Business Administration, State University of New York, Albany, NY, 1994

PROFESSIONAL EDUCATION

- Dun & Bradstreet seminar "Purchasing: A Process"
- Padgett & Thompson seminar, "Bargaining With Vendors and Suppliers"
- Keye Productivity Center seminar, "How To Be A Better Buyer"

PROFESSIONAL AFFILIATION

Member, Institute for Supply Management (formerly NAPM) since 1995

Competency-Based Functional Resume

Roger T. Cassell

3051 Mayapple Rd.
Stamford, CT 06903
203.529.0198—rtcassell@aol.com

SUMMARY

Purchasing Agent with expertise in buying equipment, office supplies, and printing services for manufacturing and financial companies. Recognized for ability to achieve cost savings, represent company interests in negotiations, and to identify low-cost vendors while ensuring high-quality service. Proven track record of:

- Achieving results
- Showing initiative
- Identifying solutions to problems
- Providing strong customer service

ACCOMPLISHMENTS

Cost Savings

- Instituted bid process for supplies and services saving company 15% annually on office supplies and 5% annually on telephone equipment.
- Saved $1,000 per month by negotiating new contract for 150 fax machines for 2,500-employee company; eliminated billing issues by including specific billing requirements in contract.
- Discontinued redundancies in purchasing by identifying preferred vendor for toner supplies; saved 12% per unit by creating first-ever bid process for toner supplies.
- Recognized for negotiating contract with printing companies that reduced business card typesetting charges from $15 to $10 per employee for 2,000 employees.
- Improved budget controls and streamlined ordering procedures by developing program for manager order approval; required departments to use assigned customer order representatives.

Customer Service

- Improved customer service by having supplies delivered to desks of department representatives; decreased lost and misdirected orders.
- Instituted weekly meetings with vendor sales representatives to improve communication about customer issues.
- Worked closely with office supplies vendor to begin quarterly "Lunch and Learn" programs for 100 customer-order representatives; accelerated resolution of customer issues and reduced returns by discussions with vendor sales representatives.
- Recognized by head of marketing department for providing outstanding customer service after negotiating for four free "same day" deliveries and improving delivery contract.

Roger T. Cassell
Page 2

ACCOMPLISHMENTS (Continued)

Negotiations
- Improved vendor pricing and service after convincing supervisors to begin bid processes for supplies and services.
- Reduced cost and administrative time by negotiating multi-year contract for company with Boise Cascade.
- Ensured company minimized downtime during change of fax machine supplier by developing scheduling timeline and conveying customer expectations.
- Facilitated meetings between 10 people at printing company and marketing, legal, and corporate communications departments to make decisions regarding business cards and stationery by deadline during corporation-wide branding change.

WORK HISTORY

R.T. Cassell Consulting, Stamford, CT   2004

IBM, New York, NY   2002–2003
Procurement Coordinator

Merrill Lynch Management Group, New York, NY   1994–2002
Purchasing Group Leader, 1997-2002
Purchasing Agent, 1994-1997

EDUCATION

B.S. in Business Administration, State University of New York, Albany, NY

Case Study: Recent Graduate

Situation

Sarah Whitehead had just graduated with a degree in finance. Even though she'd had summer internships during college, she didn't have much experience at this stage in her career. And she had not taken advantage of her college's Career Placement Office to help her get interviews during her senior year. She had expected to get an offer from the company that she had worked with during the previous summer and had been very disappointed when that did not happen.

In addition, Sarah couldn't explain what she wanted to do in a clear way. When she was asked why she had majored in finance, her response was that she had chosen finance because she "really hated accounting."

She was also concerned about her 2.9 GPA hurting her chance to be considered for some of the better jobs. Sarah had been active socially during college, and her grades had suffered. She came across as very bright, and more capable than a 2.9 GPA might indicate.

Resume Issues and Concerns

1. She had limited work experience.

2. Her GPA would not help her get interviews.

3. It was unclear what Sarah wanted to do next.

Action

The first step with Sarah was to help her figure out what she wanted to do next. We recommended some career testing for her, and spent some time asking her to explain what she liked about finance (*not* what she didn't like about accounting). It seemed to help Sarah when we talked about how most people are expected to make professional changes several times during their careers. She told me that it had been intimidating to think that she'd have to live with her decision for the rest of her career.

She decided eventually to focus on finance and try to get a corporate job. We looked at competencies online. Sarah identified the following competencies that she could demonstrate based upon some of the things she had done in school and in work assignments:

★ Analytical Thinking.

★ Achievement.

★ Impact and Influence.

★ Initiative.

★ Information Seeking.

After talking to Sarah, we discovered that she'd had some significant leadership experience during her four years in college. She'd been elected a class officer during her junior and senior years. She was a resident assistant in the dorms, and had been promoted to a hall director her senior year, managing a staff of seven resident assistants.

She could definitely demonstrate some accomplishments.

Because her education was stronger than her work experience, we recommended that the education section of her resume be first on the resume—right after the summary or profile section. After talking with Sarah, we also found out that her GPA in her major was a 3.5. Always list the highest GPA you can first, and consider leaving out GPA information for anything lower than a 3.0. Round up on the numbers—a 3.48 GPA should be listed as a 3.5 GPA. In this case, Sarah's grades may be less important to employers because of the strong reputation of Wharton at the Univeristy of Pennsylvania.

Result

Sarah's competency-based chronological resume is on page 112 and her competency-based direct resume is included on page 113. She understands that she will need to go back and tailor the resumes to focus first on the competency needs of the company she's applying to.

She became an effective competency-based networker, and had begun interviewing for positions when this book was submitted to the publisher.

She's a good candidate and has gained confidence because she knows her own competencies.

Using a competency-based resume works well for recent college graduates who want to work for organizations using competency-based systems. Sarah, who wanted to work in finance for a major company that would offer a strong training program, will benefit from having a competency-based resume. Remember that roughly 50 percent of the Fortune 500 companies use competency-based applications to help manage their human resources activities, including screening and interviewing employees.

Competency-Based Chronological Resume

Sarah Whitehead

334 Old Mystic St.   781-555-0135
Medford, MA 02155   sarahtw@yahoo.com

Profile

Financial Analyst with experience as an intern analyzing food and tobacco corporations and auditing retail brokerage offices. BSE in finance and accounting, Wharton, University of Pennsylvania, 2004. Recognized for ability to think analytically, exceed goals, persuade and influence others, and develop effective working relationships with managers, coworkers and employees. Fluent in Spanish with basic conversational skills in French and Italian.

Education

Bachelor of Science in Economics, June 2004
The Wharton School, University of Pennsylvania, Philadelphia, PA
Major: Finance   Minor: Accounting   GPA: 3.5 in Finance and Accounting

Experience

Paine Webber, Weehawken, NJ   Summer 2003
Equity Research Intern
- Selected as one of 10 summer interns for Paine Webber's New Jersey offices.
- Assisted analyst covering tobacco stocks to develop quantitative model to predict stock performance when impacted by weather conditions.
- Conducted research and analyzed results on three food stocks, prepared PowerPoint presentation and presented results to five managers and division vice president.

Merrill Lynch, Austin, TX   Summer 2002
Intern – Private Client Group
- Analyzed 20 client portfolios and prepared investment recommendations.

Charles Schwab, Austin, TX   Summer 2001
Auditing Intern – Branch Review
- Assisted Senior Controls Analyst in conducting evaluations of risk within retail sales and marketing branch offices for 10 branch offices based in Texas.

Other Information

- Voted Senior Class President and Junior Class Vice President.
- Raised $50,000 for American Heart Association as chair of dance marathon, 2003.
- Promoted to become one of 12 residence hall directors after one year as resident assistant; managed seven resident assistants and five graduate students working as night monitors.
- Earned 30% of cost of attending college through work-study and internships.

Direct Competency Resume

Sarah Whitehead

334 Old Mystic St.   781-555-0135
Medford, MA 02155   sarahtw@yahoo.com

Profile

Financial Analyst with experience as an intern analyzing food and tobacco corporations and auditing retail brokerage offices. BSE in finance and accounting, Wharton, University of Pennsylvania, 2004. Recognized for ability to think analytically, exceed goals, persuade and influence, and develop effective working relationships with others. Fluent in Spanish with basic conversational skills in French and Italian.

Education

Bachelor of Science in Economics, June 2004
The Wharton School, University of Pennsylvania, Philadelphia, PA
Major: Finance   Minor: Accounting   GPA: 3.5 in Finance and Accounting

Accomplishments

Analytical Thinking

- Assisted analyst at Paine Webber covering tobacco stocks to develop quantitative model to predict stock performance when impacted by varied economic conditions.
- Conducted research and analyzed results on three food stocks; prepared PowerPoint presentation and presented results to five senior managers and vice president.
- Analyzed 20 client portfolios and prepared investment recommendations for review.
- Completed 30-page analysis of advantages/disadvantages of financial quantitative models used by Fortune 500 for senior thesis; received A from professor.
- Assisted Senior Controls Analyst in conducting evaluations of risk within retail sales and marketing branch offices for 10 branch offices based in Texas.

Achieve Results

- Raised $50,000 for American Heart Association as chair, dance marathon, 2003.
- Promoted to one of 12 residence hall directors after year as resident assistant; managed eight resident assistants and five graduate student night monitors.
- Earned 30% of overall cost of attending college through work-study, housing office positions, and summer internships.

Influence Others

- Voted Class President, 2003 and Class Vice President, 2002, U of Pennsylvania.
- Convinced class officers to support university president after tuition increased 15%.
- Persuaded student with mental health issues to postpone serious action and see university's counseling director when working as resident assistant in dormitory.

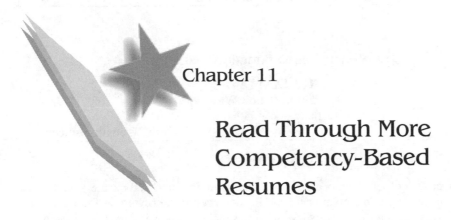

Chapter 11

Read Through More Competency-Based Resumes

When actors study for their parts, they try to *become* their character. If they are playing a part that has been played by another actor, they try to study what the other person has done with their voice and their other nonverbal communication to make the character come alive—before they put their own interpretation on the character and *become* him or her.

You can learn a lot from paying close attention to how other people do things— particularly people who do things well. Look through the resumes we've included in this chapter. Read through them and notice how they look. Which layout will work the most effectively for the person making the decision to interview you? Even though all good competency-based resumes consider the needs of the employers first, one part of that is making a decision about how you want the resume to look.

In this chapter we've given you some choices. The examples are from different professional areas, and are designed so that some of them have a slightly different look than you may be used to. We recommend demonstrating that you can use your analytical thinking competency and figure out what each person is trying to communicate to the decision-maker in their resume.

Read the summaries and profile sections first. Do you understand what the candidate is trying to emphasize? Look at the language used in the accomplishment statements. Do you see phrases that you could use when you write your own resume?

To paraphrase Confucius in the quote we used to open Chapter 10, imitation is the easiest way to become wise. The comedian Fred Allen had another saying about imitation. He said, "Imitation is the sincerest form of television."

Both men were obviously gifted in terms of their ability to use words in a way that can make us think—or just make us laugh. Pay attention to the words used in the resumes in this section. We'd be very happy to have you use these phrases or layouts or accomplishment statements. It's fine to use some of the examples in this book as models. Just remember to tailor them and make them your own. Remember that you will be a good employee, and someone will be lucky to have you working in their organization.

It's time to study the resumes included in this chapter.

Competency-Based Functional Resume

WILLIAM LIM
15415 Oak Hollow Way
Atlanta, GA 33038

770.304.1233   willmartin2@email.msn.com

SUMMARY

Plant Manager with expertise in operations, engineering, international business, and sales. Experienced in product manufacturing. Recognized for improving profitability, productivity, quality, and safety statistics. Strengths include producing results, making sound business decisions, and building effective teams. Six Sigma Green Belt. Managed team achieving ISO 9002 certification at plant. Fluent in Spanish.

ACCOMPLISHMENTS

Operations/Engineering/Maintenance
- Increased productivity eight points and reduced scrap 30% in one year by adding statistical tools, reporting systems and in-process auditing, changing inspection methods, and motivating employees by developing internal competition with prize.
- Worked closely with design engineer to take new product from conception to manufacturing; added $2 million in sales in first two years on market.

International Business
- Managed start up and growth of successful joint venture manufacturing and trading engine parts in Spain and Poland; directed activities of 70 employees.
- Recognized by senior management for troubleshooting difficult business issues; resolved quality, billing, sales, and legal issues for divisions in Norway and Ireland.

General Management/Sales
- Managed sales, operations, accounting, and engineering for engineering products plant in Memphis, TN, producing $3 million in annual sales.
- Increased sales of tubes 30%; introduced three categories of parts, reduced price and ensured on-time delivery by carrying extra inventory; decreased cost from $97 to $76 per earned hour.

WORK HISTORY

GBK Products, Atlanta, GA, and Dayton, OH   **1999–2004**
Plant Manager

PRIDE International, Atlanta, GA   **1989–1999**
Plant Manager, 1997–1999
Director, Manufacturing, 1992–1997
Plant Engineer, 1989–1992

EDUCATION

B.S. Mechanical Engineering, Georgia Institute of Technology, Atlanta, GA

Direct Competency Resume

LARRY M. HARDING, CPA
6565 Princeton Avenue
San Francisco, CA 94109
                510.555.3232
LarryMH@jps.net

SUMMARY

Financial manager with broad background in accounting, with recognized expertise in federal taxation. Certified Public Accountant. Proven ability to establish and direct efficient tax department. Experience includes progressively increasing responsibility in financial management and tax auditing. Proven track record of consistent savings in tax compliance and planning. Demonstrated strengths in research, tax analysis, disposition of corporate assets, and problem-solving. Consistent, successful completion of corporate audits. Experience in international tax laws and legislative compliance issues.

ACCOMPLISHMENTS

Research	Researched information for Ohio-Pacific International to resolve 2002 dispute with IRS over tax code 199.1. Investigated tax shelters, made recommendations to minimize tax burden, and thoroughly prepared eight subsidiary tax returns.
Reporting	Recognized for streamlining tax reporting for company in 2001 and developing first company executive summary of tax reports.
	Reviewed and filed 35 federal, state, and international returns for corporation and subsidiaries on time for 10-year period unless it was financially advantageous to ask for extension.
Problem-Solving	Created record retention system to provide accessible information in future audits in 2004; expected to reduce chance of tax penalties.
Leadership	Led industry effort to lobby for different interpretation of tax code 1155.3 to enable competition in global markets.
	Designed international tax tracking system in 2003; improved accuracy of earnings forecasting and speed of estimated tax calculations.
Strategic Thinking	Directed transition team during phase-out of tax services after takeover, April 2004. Worked closely with Chief Legal Officer from acquiring company to anticipate problems and ensure compliance with tax codes during transition.
	Directed internal tax audit to better evaluate impact of proposed state tax changes on company tax burden.
International Perspective	Developed first company-wide international tax accounting system during 1997 acquisition of company operating in France, Germany, Australia, and Brazil.
	Improved working relationship with European subsidiaries after researching country tax codes, meeting with five country tax managers and allowing group to develop recommendations on how to best handle tax reporting to corporate office.

Larry M. Harding

EMPLOYMENT HISTORY

OHIO-PACIFIC INTERNATIONAL *1993–2004*
   Senior Manager, Tax Services, San Francisco, CA, 2003–2004
   Manager Tax Services, Cleveland, OH, 1998–2003
   Assistant Manager Tax Services, Cleveland, OH, 1993–1998

INTERNAL REVENUE, SAN FRANCISCO, CA *1983–1992*
   Manager, Financial Accounting – Compliance, 1987–1988
   Senior Analyst, Federal Income Taxes, 1986–1987
   Manager Financial Accounting – Compliance, 1985–1987
   Internal Revenue Service Audit Coordinator, 1983–1985

EDUCATION

M.B.A. Accounting and Finance
Darden Graduate School of Business Administration
University of Virginia, Charlottesville, VA

B.A. Business Administration – Finance and Accounting
University of Michigan, Ann Arbor, MI

CERTIFICATIONS

Certified Public Accountant—California, Ohio, and New York

Direct Competency Resume

Ruth R. Litten
6787 Pike Street East
Chicago, IL 60206
(312) 555-4435
RuthRLTN2@yahoo.net

SUMMARY

Civil Engineer with strengths in training engineering project managers for industrial, environmental, commercial, and residential projects. Recognized for ability to represent organization interests when negotiating with architectural/law firms and government officials. Experienced in concept development, identifying needs, preparing and presenting client proposals, preparing design drawings, and managing building processes. Lead consultant on environmental impact studies. Excellent presentation, interpersonal, and written communication skills. Fluent in Spanish.

COMPETENCIES / ACCOMPLISHMENTS

Results
- Developed first damage inspections training for U.S. Federal Emergency Management Association; trained 85 civil engineers and contractors how to write and submit reports authorizing residential building funds for reconstruction. Graduated 92% of attendees.
- Decreased annual transportation budget for firm 32% by identifying five preferred vendors and negotiating exclusive contracts.
- Coordinated eight electrical and mechanical contractors and specified/sourced materials to complete $18 million field-modification project. Project came in under budget and on time.

Impact and Influence
- Ensured continuation of crucial building construction and renovation for Ingles Mall after convincing city environmental manager to waive restrictions; saved $2 million in legal fees after negotiating with State of Illinois to eliminate requirement for wetlands environmental impact study.
- Selected to answer media questions about high profile engineering projects impacting city of Chicago and Cook County residents. Wrote official response to technical questions from affected individuals.
- Developed and delivered 20 engineering presentations to city, county, state, federal, and community agencies and organizations in 2003.

Technical Expertise
- Reduced on-the-job accidents 84% in three months after designing and delivering safety training for 20 engineers working with environmental projects; trained staff on safety issues with corrosives, toxic compounds, and nitrogen compressed gas.
- Trained five new engineers each year on drainage engineering, and engineering/flood plain analysis. Developed computer program to perform drainage analysis.
- Wrote plans, specifications, cost estimates and performed engineering studies for six months, $3.5 million hazardous waste removal project in Southern Illinois; received bonus for completing project in five months, ahead of schedule and under budget.

Ruth R. Litten   **page 2**

WORK HISTORY

Pinnacle and Point Engineering Consultants, Inc., Chicago, IL   **1998–present**
Senior Consultant Engineer - Environmental Specialist, 2000–present
Director, Civil Engineering Training and Development, 1998–2000

U.S. Environmental Protection Agency, Western Region, Dallas, TX   **1995–1998**
Civil Engineering/Environmental Management Trainer and Consultant

EDUCATION

B.S. Civil Engineering, University of Kentucky, Louisville, KY
B.S. Environmental Management, Illinois Institute for Technology, Chicago, IL

CREDENTIALS

State of Kentucky Civil Engineer No. 5566432
State of Illinois Civil Engineer No. 2234512

AFFILIATIONS

Life Member of American Society of Civil Engineers (ASCE)

Competency-Based Chronological Resume

Carla J. Hansen

344 South 9898 East Bench
Washington, DC 20002
202.551.3345
CJHOfc@Yahoo.com

Career Summary

Executive Assistant to senior managers and leaders in U.S. government. Excellent written and verbal skills, with exceptional proficiency in scheduling, planning, coordinating, and documenting special events, confidential meetings, media appearances, and conferences. Known for ability to coordinate complex events while remaining calm and organized. Strong understanding of protocol and cultural sensitivities. Excellent reputation for confidentiality and professionalism. Recognized for being expert in agency on Microsoft Word and PowerPoint. Type 90 wpm.

Software Experience

- Word
- PowerPoint
- Excel
- WordPerfect
- Flash

- Access
- Outlook
- Quicken
- Corel Draw

Work Experience

1993–present

Federal Aviation Administration, Washington, DC
Executive Administrator, 1998–present

- Coordinated aviation policy and safety awareness meetings. Scheduled 35 public sessions in 2003 to promote aviation safety.
- Recognized by Director of FAA for effectively organizing meetings with attendance of 200–300 people.
- Answered inquiries from national and local media stations in crisis situations; directed calls to managers and directors. Built strong relationships with media.
- Maintained security of critical documents and sensitive reports.
- Coordinated activities of six clerks supporting three FAA executives and six managers.
- Received excellent evaluations; recognized for maintaining organization and open communication in stressful situations.

Carla J. Hansen

Work Experience (continued)

Federal Aviation Administration (continued)
Assistant to the Executive Administrator, 1993–1998

- Produced correspondence and letters for Executive Administrator and other agency managers.
- Screened, recorded, handled, and referred 100 caller questions and inquiries per day.
- Managed production of aviation safety manuals and handout materials for 25,000 mailings each year.
- Reduced search time for contacts 75% by creating Access database to monitor, document, and catalogue mailing lists, documents, and professional contact information.

Key Competencies

- Administration and Management
- Attention to Detail
- Communications/Media Savvy
- Customer Oriented
- Technical Competence
- Office Automation

- Manage and Organize Information
- Credibility
- Verbal and Written Communication
- Organizational Awareness

Education

Associate of Arts
Miami-Dade Community College, Miami, FL

Executive Assistant Certification,
DOI University, Denver, CO

Direct Competency Resume

Mason Bennett

955 3rd Avenue   (801) 555-9268
Salt Lake City, UT 84103   MBnt@yahoo.com

Summary

Hardware engineer in digital and analog communications with experience in computer, communications, and multimedia industries. Recognized for expertise in computerized audio and signal processing. Directed team on design and implementation of PC Cards and accessories for mobile data products. Wrote and developed business case for wide area wireless data strategies/products. Strengths include technical knowledge, ability to achieve results, analytical thinking, thoroughness, and communication skills.

Specialized Technical Skills

Circuit Card Development, VHDL, PADS layout tools, Model Sim, Project 2000 Advanced, Action Science Dialogue 1 and 2, and Altera

Accomplishments

Technical Expertise

- Assisted in design of DataWare/Megahertz modem products on C52 and C54 TI-based platform implemented on DAA and 15-pin connector analog interface.

- Coordinated prototyping design work for firm, and procurement and debugging of prototype PC cards. Supported design team in analog design and testing.

- Co-designed and managed construction of microprocessor-based broadcast system for Mica-Productions.

- Designed analog/digital circuits, wrote specifications, managed 15 engineers, and developed modifications accepted as industry standard while working on IBM project.

Results

- Coordinated design efforts with four hardware engineers for development of first Desktop PC Sound Card in firm history.

- Increased product reliability 30% after recognizing need for new product testing, developing and testing procedure, and persuading senior management to use procedure.

Analytical Thinking

- Analyzed customer needs, designed prototype, and developed Megahertz brand accessory products for LAN + Modem products.

- Prepared design alternatives based on technology developments; anticipated changes required for project review.

Accomplishments (continued)

Thoroughness

- Developed product requirements, design specifications, test plans, and product documentation from conception to production for accessory products.

- Led design engineering team and won award for most projects completed on time and within budget for company.

Communication Skills

- Developed and presented 50 technical demos annually to customers and board members; consistently received positive evaluations.

- Wrote and presented design proposal for $5 million project. Directed 11 engineering team members and made adjustments because of technological needs. Recognized for completing project under budget.

Employment History

1996 – Current	**DataWare**	**Salt Lake City, UT**
	Project Lead Engineer, 1999–Current	
	Hardware Design Engineer, 1996–1999	
1997 – 1998	**BAK Technology**	**Salt Lake City, UT**
	Design/Test Engineer	
1996 – 1997	**Calson Test Group**	**Salt Lake City, UT**
	Test Engineer/Electronic Technician	

Education

B.S. Electronics Engineering Technology, 1995
Cogswell Polytechnical College, Sunnyvale, CA

- Emphasis in audio signal processing design (DSP, analog, and systems)
- Dean's List and President's List, 1995

Chapter 12

Create Competency-Based Correspondence

You've worked hard, and you know that you feel good about your new competency-based resume targeting a specific opportunity. You may be asking yourself, "What else can I do to highlight my competencies and get my resume to the top of the pile?"

But first, you need to do a few things—particularly if you are interested in getting a new job with a new organization. And in the next two chapters, we'll give you some ideas about how to conduct the rest of your job search in a more focused, competency-based way.

Thomas Jefferson said, "I'm a great believer in luck, and I find the harder I work, the more I have of it." If you are willing to work hard to get your next opportunity, you will improve your chance of getting it. Using the competency-based approach will help you work in a smarter, more targeted way to improve your success rate, but plan on working hard too.

You'll need good cover and thank you letters, strong networking skills and the ability to interview effectively. In many cases, you can expect your interviewer to use behavioral questions targeted to determine your expertise in the competencies the organization cares about. If you are interested in a new position within your current organization, you may be able to apply without having to provide a cover letter.

Remember that even Cinderella needed to get her prince to choose her once she went to the ball. And if the story hasn't changed, her foot had to be the perfect fit for the glass slipper once he decided he was interested. The good news is that your resume, correspondence, and networking and interviewing skills don't disappear at midnight. We promise.

In this chapter, we're going to focus on how to write competency-based cover letters and thank you notes. They will support the resume and can help the employer better understand what you are trying to sell.

We'll explain what makes competency-based correspondence different and more effective, and give you a few examples of letters for you to look at. In today's job market, it is important to realize that most correspondence is now happening over the Internet. While you still need to use your judgment, plan on most cover letters and thank you notes being online—unless you know that the decision-maker is more comfortable with the older, hard copy approach.

Competency-Based Cover Letters

Even though their resume may be strong, we've seen people who weren't selected for interviews because their cover letter was not written well. Many candidates don't understand what happens to their resumes once they are submitted.

If the organization uses screening software, the resumes are first screened to determine who best matches the criteria for the position by who has the highest matching level with the *keywords* identified by the manager or human resources professionals involved. Most human resources professionals divide resumes into the "yes," "no," and "maybe" stacks and rarely return to the maybes. They then read the cover letters attached to resumes in the "yes" stack as a way to help them pick the strongest qualified candidates to bring in for interviews.

The cover letter, in essence, are less important than the resume because most recruiters and human resources professionals will only take the time to read them when they've determined that you are qualified for the position—based on the resume. But they can make a difference in some cases and can cause you to be completely eliminated if the cover letter is not well written.

One format that works well for most people when writing a cover letter is explained on page 127.

First step: If you've been referred by someone the person you're sending the letter to knows, start off by telling them who referred you and how you know the person. If not, begin with identifying the position you are interested in and explain where you heard about the opportunity.

Second step: Tell the reader how you meet his needs. If you've written a competency-based resume, you should be able to identify the organization's needs much more clearly after doing a little research because you understand the competencies it is looking for. Discuss the competencies you have that match what the organization is looking for. Give the reader an example of a recent accomplishment that demonstrates expertise with one of the most critical competencies for his organization's success.

Third step: Let the reader know what you want him to do. Make sure that you tell him that you have attached a resume for his review and look forward to talking with him in the near future. Mention that you will follow up and contact him in the next week (if this is appropriate). Thank him for his time and consideration.

Sample Competency-Based Cover Letter

Ad Response for Sales Manager Position

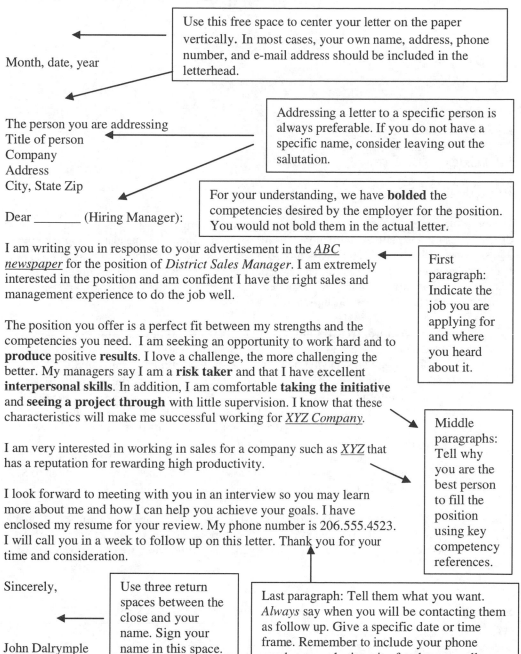

Month, date, year

Use this free space to center your letter on the paper vertically. In most cases, your own name, address, phone number, and e-mail address should be included in the letterhead.

The person you are addressing
Title of person
Company
Address
City, State Zip

Addressing a letter to a specific person is always preferable. If you do not have a specific name, consider leaving out the salutation.

Dear _____ (Hiring Manager):

For your understanding, we have **bolded** the competencies desired by the employer for the position. You would not bold them in the actual letter.

I am writing you in response to your advertisement in the *ABC newspaper* for the position of *District Sales Manager*. I am extremely interested in the position and am confident I have the right sales and management experience to do the job well.

First paragraph: Indicate the job you are applying for and where you heard about it.

The position you offer is a perfect fit between my strengths and the competencies you need. I am seeking an opportunity to work hard and to **produce** positive **results**. I love a challenge, the more challenging the better. My managers say I am a **risk taker** and that I have excellent **interpersonal skills**. In addition, I am comfortable **taking the initiative** and **seeing a project through** with little supervision. I know that these characteristics will make me successful working for *XYZ Company*.

I am very interested in working in sales for a company such as *XYZ* that has a reputation for rewarding high productivity.

Middle paragraphs: Tell why you are the best person to fill the position using key competency references.

I look forward to meeting with you in an interview so you may learn more about me and how I can help you achieve your goals. I have enclosed my resume for your review. My phone number is 206.555.4523. I will call you in a week to follow up on this letter. Thank you for your time and consideration.

Sincerely,

Use three return spaces between the close and your name. Sign your name in this space.

John Dalrymple

Enclosure

Last paragraph: Tell them what you want. *Always* say when you will be contacting them as follow up. Give a specific date or time frame. Remember to include your phone number to make it easier for them to call you.

Sample Competency-Based Cover Letter

Jim A. Brophy
5515 Echo Road, Salt Lake City, UT 84102
801-555-4387
JBPHY@yahoo.com

June 9, 20XX

R. L. Walker
PermStor
2318 Nesbitt Road
Salt Lake City, Utah 84101

RE: International Sales Manager Position

I am a results-oriented sales professional—sales instructor, marketing manager, and district sales representative—with more than 10 years experience in management, marketing and sales training. I have been consistently recognized as one of the top producers in sales in every organization I've worked for, and have developed effective long-term working relationships with key customers. My experience can help PermStor open new markets, develop strong customer relationships, and increase sales.

- **I have developed, written, and instructed sales seminars and courses**. In fact, I am scheduled to be a presenter at the Canadian International Sales Expo this September. I will be speaking on the topic of sales and relationship building.
- **My strengths are forecasting, customer relationships, negotiating, and consensus building**.
  - One of the most significant projects that I worked on was negotiating a unique rental package agreement for storage units that is projected to net a profit of $2 million in the next three years.
  - At James Company I was responsible for managing five key customer relationships. I helped build the associated revenue from $7.5 million to $12 million in two years.

I am confident that my experience and drive are what you are looking for at PermStor. If you have any questions or I can provide any additional information, please contact me at (801) 555-4387. I will contact you in the near future to arrange a time when we could discuss the position further.

Sincerely,

Jim A. Brophy

Enclosure

Don't expect to write one cover letter and have it work well for you in every situation. No one wants to receive a canned letter, and most human resources professionals and recruiters can recognize a standardized letter when they see one. The real difference in following the competency-based approach is that you can't use a canned letter, because you need to specifically target the employer's needs. If you care about the position, take the time to write a cover letter that specifically targets the opportunity.

Use your judgment when writing cover letters. Each situation may be a little different and require different language or ideas. For example, if you are responding to an advertisement, clearly respond to the requirements or competencies listed in the ad. Tailor your letters for each situation. Try to match the language, terminology, and tone you've seen in company publications and on the Website, if you can.

Look through some books that discuss how to write effective cover letters to get more examples and tips. Two books that might give you additional ideas are *Cover Letters! Cover Letters! Cover Letters!* by Richard Fein (Career Press, 1997) and *Last Minute Cover Letters* by Brandon Toropov (Career Press, 1998). Remember that these books will give you some good ideas about how to write cover letters; you still will need to tailor your letters to the new, competency-based way discussed in the second step (page 126).

Thank You Notes

We've also seen candidates be eliminated because of the thank you notes they sent. In general, it is better not to send a thank you note than to send a poorly written one.

But a well-written thank you note *can* make a difference and help you receive a second interview or even an offer. It can give the hiring manager an idea about the quality of work that you can do, so take the time to make it stand out.

One candidate for a computer geoscience position took the time to write six distinct thank you letters to his individual interviewers at a company. The hiring manager was so impressed that he went to the other five interviewers, compared the letters to confirm how well written and unique each letter was, and made the candidate an offer.

That candidate did a particularly effective job of including a sentence or two about what the interviewer said or what they talked about that had most impressed him.

We encourage you to take that same approach of listening very carefully during the interview or networking conversation for specific comments that you can later include in your thank you notes. You can also include a sentence talking about your competencies or skills that may not have been emphasized in the interview—and explain how they could benefit the company.

If you are writing a thank you note for an interview, also try to subtly let the interviewer know that you are strong in the competencies her organization is looking for. At the end of the note, let the interviewer know that you are genuinely interested in the position.

Make sure that you write the thank you notes to the right people and that you've spelled their names correctly. Remember to ask for a business card from the networking contact or the interviewer.

You wouldn't have wanted to be the candidate whose potential manager, Suzanne, came to the human resources professional and showed her the thank you note the candidate had sent to her secretary, Susan, thinking that she was the manager. That candidate did *not* get a second interview.

Take the time to write a well-written, competency-based thank you note. It can make a difference.

Send the thank you notes within 24 hours of your interview. In today's business environment, sending a thank you note by e-mail is perfectly appropriate in most situations.

Remember that e-mails are date and time stamped—don't send them immediately after returning home because you can appear desperate, or between midnight and 6 a.m. because you might be perceived differently than you are intending. Never send *any correspondence* related to looking for a job outside your current organization from your account with your current employer.

Spell-check the thank you note, and review it carefully for grammatical and usage mistakes.

Writing effective cover letters and thank you notes, when done with quality and accuracy, will give you another big edge in your job search. Remember to target the competencies you identified in all of your correspondence; use competency-based language whenever possible.

Key Points for Chapter 12	
"In all human affairs there are efforts, and there are results, and the strength of effort is the measure of the results." —James Allen	
Key Questions	**Answers**
How should I submit my cover and thank you letters?	Use your good judgment, but plan on most cover letters and thank you notes being online in today's environment.
Would you give me a cover letter checklist to follow?	*Customize your letter for each position and organization you are applying for.*

Key Points for Chapter 12(continued)	
Key Questions	**Answers**
	Follow this checklist when writing your cover letter:
	1. Identify the position you are interested in. Tell them where you heard about the opportunity or who gave you the referral. *Paragraph 1*
	2. Discuss the competencies you have that match what they are looking for. Give them an example of a recent accomplishment that demonstrates expertise with one of the most critical competencies. *Paragraph 2*
	3. Summarize your letter. *Paragraph 3* • Tell the reader what you want them to do. • Tell them that you have attached a resume for their review • Tell them you look forward to talking with them in the near future. • Mention that you will follow up and contact them in the next week. • Thank them for their time/consideration.
	4. Edit your resume. *Final review* • On hard copies, check for visual appeal and white space. • Check grammar and spelling. • Check for proper business letter format. • Check for the tone and quality of communication.
Why should I write a thank you letter?	If you are being seriously considered for a position, writing a thank you note will help your potential employer view you in a more positive way. It might be the final piece of information that lands you the position. It gives you an opportunity to mention anything you may have missed during your interview. It gives you the chance to market yourself one last time. If you are in the final running, it helps them make the decision in your favor.

Chapter 13

Prepare for Competency-Based Networking and Interviewing

Most career consultants agree that the purpose of the resume is to get an interview; and the purpose of the interview is to get a job offer.

The job search process is a little like fishing. You get the bait and the fishing rods ready, and then you go to the water, bait your hook, cast the line, and hopefully get a bite. Depending on the size of the fish, you may need help reeling in the line and catching the fish in the net.

This chapter is going to give you the right *fishing* equipment, or tools, so that you can successfully network, interview, and land the best job opportunity. We'll give you tips to help you reel in the right position—the more effective competency-based way.

Networking the Competency-Based Way

Politicians, sales professionals, and fundraisers become successful because they build a strong network with people and follow through to ask for what they want—the vote, the sale, or a major donation.

Networking, very simply, is getting out, and meeting and talking with people for a purpose. Competency-based networking, by telephone or in person, helps you find out information about the position you are interested in and the competencies required to be successful on the job. We're going to give you some basic tips to help you network with purpose so you can talk to the people who can help you figure out what kind of fish are in the pond, how big the pond is, and what kind of lure will be the most attractive for the *right* fish.

1. Network with purpose. Talk with people until you've found someone who knows the "inside story" about the competencies the organization is looking for and is willing to share that information. Ask questions to see if you can gain insight that can help you convince the decision-makers in the organization that they should interview you. In other words, you need to be marketing yourself and your competencies—even while networking.

2. Be persistent when you are networking, but don't be a pest. Delphia York Duckens, vice president of fundraising and brand management for the Girl Scouts organization in Houston, says that she routinely does not accept no as an answer from prospective donors—until they've said it at least three times.

3. Remember that your network of people is much larger than you think it is. You know people from your work, your neighborhood, your family and friends, your religious group, your doctors and dentists, your alumni organizations, your children's contacts through school or sports, and your own activities. Each of these contacts knows other people, and most would be happy to introduce you to them. Most career consultants agree that we should all have about 250 people in our network at any time, and should always be making an effort to add to the list.

4. Don't be too proud to ask for help. You need people on the inside who will help advocate for you.

 Hint: You may need to shift your attitude. It is always interesting for us to do a training program and find out how many people are really uncomfortable with the idea of asking for help. We ask them if they've ever helped someone else get a new job or promotion—and how they felt about it. They almost always tell us that they felt good about helping. We then explain to them that if they refuse to ask someone else for help, they are denying that person the chance to feel good about helping *them.*

5. When you talk to networking contacts with a strong contact inside the organization, remember that one of your goals is to win an advocate for you. Give them a copy of your resume and promote what you have done related to the competencies identified for the position. Ask for his help.

6. Remember to thank your contacts at the end of the conversation for their help and advice. Offer to reciprocate by asking if there's anything you can do for them. Send e-mails thanking them for their help the following morning.

7. Follow through and remember to let your contacts know what happens as a result of the contact or information they provided. Stay in touch periodically. Most people do not appreciate it when they are only contacted when someone is looking for a new job. They'll usually help you once and maybe twice. You need to nurture your network. This is an opportunity to show your level of social sophistication.

For more information on networking effectively, we recommend the book *Power Networking, Second Edition* by Donna Fisher and Sandy Vilas (Bard Press, 2000). Always remember to take the best of the ideas from other sources and add the new idea of networking to find out about competencies. Remember to promote how your own competencies are a *fit* for the position. Encourage the contact to help support you, or advocate for you, within his or her own network.

Interviewing Success in Behavioral Interviews

Preparing an effective competency-based resume *will* also help you be more successful with behavioral interviews. If you've written a competency-based resume, you've already thought about the competencies required for the position and about how your accomplishments demonstrate that you have some expertise with these competencies. Because you now understand the importance of matching your background to the organization's needs, you will have an advantage when you are answering behavioral interview questions.

Most competency-based organizations use behavioral interviewing as their main interviewing style. Behavioral interviews are based on the theory that past behavior is the best predictor of future behavior. Past behavior predicts future success. Typically, interviewers ask questions to find out how the candidate has behaved in the past in the key areas required to be successful on the job. Do you see the connection to competencies?

Some organizations use highly structured behavioral interviews (that is, targeted selection interviews) that provide interviewers with a list of questions to choose from in each competency identified for the position. In the table on page 136, we've given you at least one example of a behavioral question for each of the most widely used competencies.

So what's the best advice on how you can prepare for a behavioral interview?

1. Review the competencies for the position. Make sure you understand what the organization is looking for.

2. Reread your resume. Pay particular attention to the accomplishment statements you wrote to show how your background "matches" the competencies the organization needs. Know which accomplishment statement describes what you have done in each competency area.

3. Make sure you can answer questions about each accomplishment statement— in depth. Review the details about projects you worked on a few years ago so that you can come across as credible. Be able to talk about the results of the project—including specifics about cost or deadlines. Understand how the project had a positive impact on the organization.

Competency	Behavioral Question
Results Orientation	Tell me about a time that you were goal-oriented. Describe your most challenging sale.
Initiative	Describe a situation at work where you had to be particularly persistent. Have you anticipated and prepared for a future problem that is not obvious to others? Tell me about it.
Impact/Influence	Tell me about a time that you persuaded your managers or clients to change their minds about a business decision. Have you ever built "behind-the scenes" support for your ideas or influenced indirectly? Tell me about it.
Customer Service Orientation	Describe a situation where you went "above and beyond the call" for one of your clients or customers.
Interpersonal Understanding	Tell me about a situation where your awareness of nonverbal communication or the underlying issues helped you resolve a problem (or sense an opportunity). If you've worked with different cultures, please describe a situation where your multicultural sensitivity caused you to change your own approach to reach the business goal.
Organizational Awareness	Tell me about a time when understanding the organization's politics helped you do a better job.
Analytical Thinking	Describe the steps you went through to manage and complete the project.
Conceptual Thinking	Have you created any new concepts or models based upon recognizing patterns or trends? Would you please describe the thinking process you went through?
Information Seeking	Tell me about an assignment you worked on where you had to be resourceful and dig for information.
Integrity	Describe a situation where you had to make a difficult decision based upon your values.

4. Identify other accomplishments related to the competency list for the position. Try to have at least one example to talk about for each competency.

5. Remember that most interviewers who have been through behavioral interview training are going to evaluate your answers and listen to see if you included a description of the situation or problem, the action you took, and the result of the action (or benefit to the organization).

6. Expect most of your questions to be behavioral, but don't be surprised if some aren't.

Remember that the purpose of the resume is to get an interview, and the purpose of the interview is to get a job. Being savvy enough to be able to explain how your accomplishments prove that you are competent in the areas the organization needs will first, give you an edge in getting the interview, and second, help ensure that you get that job offer.

It is also important to be aware that interviewers, in general, are looking for three major things in all candidates:

1. Can you do the job? Do you have the right skills, experience, education, or credentials?

2. Will you do the job? Are you motivated and willing to work hard?

3. Will you *fit* in the department and organization? Do you have good communication and interpersonal skills? Will other people be willing to work with you?

In addition to being prepared for a competency-based behavioral interview, you also need to interview well. We'll give you a quick review of some of the same basic tips we'd give to any candidate getting ready for any interview, and give you tips we *haven't* covered when we talked about preparing for behavioral interviews.

1. Prepare for the interview. In addition to knowing how your accomplishments match the organization's needs, take the time to research the organization. Look at the Website and get the financial information. Know the details about the organization including what product it makes or service it delivers. Find out how many employees work there and try to figure out what kind of culture the organization has. Talk to the people in your network and find out the "real story" about the organization.

2. Know how you plan to answer typical questions such as:
   ★ Tell me about yourself.
   ★ What are your biggest strengths?
   ★ What is your biggest weakness?
   ★ Why are you interested in this position?

For more information on how to answer these questions turn to Appendix G.

3. Get a reasonable amount of sleep the night before the interview.

4. Create the *right* first impression. Remember that the interviewer's perception matters and that most interviewers make up their minds very quickly in the interview.

    Look professional for the interview. Dress appropriately for the position—but if you are not sure, you are generally safer dressing conservatively. We would always tell a banker to dress in a dark business suit for an interview but know that a creative manager interviewing with an advertising agency might be able to dress a little less conservatively. If you are not sure, ask your contacts within the organization for recommendations. Recruiters, human resources professionals, or managers you know should be able to help you. Take the time to make sure your hair and nails look groomed and that your shoes have been shined recently and have good heels.

    Get to your interview early but wait to go to the lobby and have the receptionist call the interviewer until 5 to 10 minutes before the interview. It can be just as annoying to an interviewer for a candidate to arrive 30 minutes early as 30 minutes late.

    Unless you are Yao Ming or Shaquille O'Neal's height, avoid sitting down in the lobby while you are waiting for your interviewer—most of us look more professional standing up. When the interviewer arrives, make sure you smile and use direct eye contact and a firm handshake.

5. During the interview, be articulate and positive. Stay focused on what you want out of the interview: a second interview or a job offer. Answer questions in a positive way—avoid saying things that make the interviewer perceive you as a victim. Let the interviewer take the lead—we've seen some candidates get into serious trouble by trying to take the interview over from the interviewer. If you are asked a difficult question, pause and think through your answer before you start talking.

    Listen to the question and respond to the question being asked. Most interviewers do not want to hire someone who demonstrates during the interview that they do not do a good job of listening. Ask an occasional question during the interview to show the interviewer that you are listening and genuinely interested in the work.

    Pay attention to your nonverbal communication. Make sure that you are talking loud enough, maintaining eye contact, and sitting up straight. Don't lean back—it can be interpreted as a lack of interest. If you lean slightly too far forward, the interviewer may just think you are invading his space and are socially inept.

6. Expect to be asked if you have any questions at the end of the interview. This is one of those unwritten rules: **you need to have questions**. If you don't, the interviewer will assume you are not interested in the position. So what are good questions to ask? The best questions are those that show interest in the work you are being hired to do. You also can win points by asking a follow-up question to

something the interviewer told you during the interview, because it will demonstrate that you are listening and that you are flexible enough to ask about something you clearly could not have planned to ask about.

 Hint: One good question: "When you think about the person who has been the most successful in this position, what did they do the first few months to be so successful?" See if you can identify her competencies from the interviewer's answer.

7. At the end of the interview, the interviewer should explain what you could expect as the next step. If the interviewer doesn't tell you, ask "What's the next step?" Remember to tell the interviewer that you are very interested in the position and thank the interviewer for his time.

We recommend that you take some time to read through some books to get additional ideas on how to improve your interview skills. Kate Wendleton's *Interviewing and Salary Negotiation* (Career Press, 1999) and Martin Yate's *Knock 'Em Dead 2004: Great Answers to Over 200 Tough Interview Questions* (Adams Media, 2003) are two good places to start.

Key Points for Chapter 13		
"No man can fight his way to the top and stay at the top without exercising the fullest measure of grit, courage, determination, and resolution." —B.C. Forbes		
Key Questions	**Answers**	
What is networking?	Networking is getting out, meeting, and talking with people for a purpose.	
What is the process for successful networking?	Network with a purpose.	• Know what you want to know. • Know who you want to meet. • Know what you want to market.
	Be persistent but don't be a pest.	• Know what you would like and ask for it in a number of ways. • Ask if they know of anyone they can recommend for you to talk to.
	Know that your network is bigger than you think.	• All the people you do business with are part of your network. • Everyone you know socially is part of your network. • People you have known, worked with, or gone to school with in the past are part of your network.
	Don't be afraid to ask for what you want.	• You must know what you want before you start contacting people in your network.

Key Points for Chapter 13 (continued)

Key Questions	Answers	
	Understand it is important to nurture your network.	• Always ask if there is something you can do for them. What you give, you get back. • Keep in contact with your network; nurture your network by keeping in touch even when you don't need anything. • Get help from people, and win them as an advocate for you. • Always thank the people in your network for the help they give you. • Let the people in your network know how they have helped you in your job search.
What is a behavioral question?	A behavioral question asks you to give examples of what you have done in a particular situation in the past.	Examples of behavioral questions are: • Tell me when you were able to achieve results under stressful circumstances. • Describe what you did in your past organization to improve morale. When responding to behavioral questions use these steps: • Describe the situation or **P**roblem. • Tell about the **A**ction you took to change or improve the situation. • Describe the **R**esult or outcome. Remember to use the competencies as your guide in choosing your responses. Choose situations that match the competencies you need to demonstrate.
How do I prepare for an interview?	• Create the right first impression. Dress for success. • Plan and rehearse answers to the typical interview questions. • Remember the competency list you made for the position and answer questions based on the organization's needs. • Have questions to ask at the end of the interview. Listen during the interview for things that you can ask questions about at the end of the interview. Try to include some competency-based questions.	

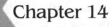

Chapter 14

The Next Step: Actively Manage Your Career in a Competency-Based Organization

Congratulations! You wrote an extremely effective competency-based resume and got the position you wanted at the competency-based organization. Now what do you do?

If you don't pick up the signs that the organization you're now working for evaluates and rewards their employees differently than you may be used to seeing, you may not thrive in the new culture. It is critical that you understand the organization's culture and the competencies you'll be measured against as soon as possible after starting your new job. You'll need to learn what you can do to ensure you will be perceived as successful by your new managers in the competency-based system.

When we were in school, most of us learned that our teachers gave higher grades to the students who made the effort to understand their assignments and deliver the product the teachers expected to receive. But sometimes people don't want to follow the instructions and don't seem to understand that succeeding is usually based upon delivering what your teachers and managers expect you to deliver.

One student told his professor that he should be rewarded for putting in the extra effort to develop and deliver a 10-minute speech instead of the five-minute speech he'd been assigned! Even though the instructor gave him some credit for being creative and coming up with a novel explanation, she still took some points off—for not following instructions.

Most of us have learned the hard way that if we "buck the system," there are consequences that we may not like. While it is important to understand how the system works and to work within the system, it is also important for us (and our organizations) to work with integrity and to feel good about the work that we do. After all, integrity is a rising star on the list of competencies in U.S. organizations.

Recognizing the role of competencies in certain organizations and learning to promote your competencies and your career with your managers *will* make a tremendous difference in your career.

You've taken the first step toward managing your career in a competency-based organization by identifying the competencies for the position. Secondly, you've developed accomplishment statements to showcase your value in each competency area. Next, you've put together an effective competency-based resume that helped the hiring managers realize how their organization could benefit from having you as an employee. And finally, you've learned how to answer behavioral questions about your expertise in critical competencies.

By going through these steps, you've also gained some communication competencies. As you continue developing your career, you should constantly be aware of building, tracking, and mastering key competencies.

If you've been savvy enough to read through this book, we're going to make an assumption that you are open to some coaching and want to continue developing as an employee, receiving the rewards, and moving up in your career.

To help you be perceived as a star in your organization, we've got seven main suggestions for you:

1. Set up and use a system to track your competencies and accomplishments.

2. Keep your competency-based resume updated.

3. Develop your critical competencies to a higher level.

4. Identify and overcome your competency gaps.

5. Add new competencies that might be critical in future positions.

6. Promote your career by making sure your managers know your competencies.

7. Submit an updated list of your latest accomplishments to your manager before each performance appraisal. Update your resume to be ready for new opportunities.

Set up and use a system to track your competencies and accomplishments.

It is important to have a system to keep track of your competencies and any accomplishments that demonstrate these competencies. Whether you use a spreadsheet program such as MS Excel or a database program such as Access, you should include accomplishments related to the competencies identified for your current position and competencies for positions you are interested in being considered for in the future. More details about how to set up this kind of tracking system are included in Chapter 8.

Keep your competency-based resume updated.

When you start a new job, it is very easy to focus on the work and not take the time to make sure you are prepared for the future. While different time frames work well for different people, we recommend that you update your resume every three to six months based upon the competencies identified for your current position.

Develop your critical competencies to a higher level.

Look for opportunities to develop the competencies identified for your current job so that you can show accomplishments and overall performance at a higher level. During your performance appraisal, pay particular attention to competencies identified as "developmental needs."

How do you build your competencies? Ask for assignments that will enable you to develop accomplishments in a particular competence area. Find a mentor or coach to help you.

Identify relevant training programs—inside your organization, in the community, and at colleges and universities. Look for opportunities to develop your competencies inside and outside your work environment. Many employees are involved with volunteer work or teach classes at a university or college, and are able to build their competencies, especially "Impact and Influence," "Analytical or Conceptual Thinking," and "Customer Service Orientation." You can too.

 Hint: You might be in a junior-level human resources position where "Customer Service Orientation" is an important competency. Your manager has evaluated your performance as being effective with follow-up and maintaining clear communication. To develop your "Customer Service Orientation" competency to a higher level, you need to demonstrate that you take personal responsibility, make yourself fully available, and act to make things better.

As you get more senior in your career and move up the organization, you'd be expected to use a long-term perspective, and act as a trusted adviser or client advocate. Ask for assignments and look for opportunities to demonstrate that you've done work at a higher level, and write accomplishment statements to prove it.

Identify and overcome your competency gaps.

Sometimes your weakest competency areas can become your biggest opportunities for growth. These are the *competency gaps* that need to be bridged and overcome.

What competencies are you being evaluated against that you know you cannot prove that you have? Perception matters.

Someone who just transferred into sales from engineering may not be rated at as high a level on Customer Service Orientation as a sales professional who'd spent his career in sales. But the former engineer may bring strengths in some other areas that make him an asset to the department. If he's going to be a good fit for the sales department, he'll look for opportunities to overcome the competency gaps he's identified, and do it within the first few months on the job. In this particular scenario, in addition to training, a mentor or coach would be a tremendous help.

Add new competencies that might be critical in future positions.

In addition to the competencies that you need to be monitoring and tracking on your current job, you need to be planning for the future. What kind of work would you like to be doing in the next five or 10 years? Which competencies are critical for those positions? What level of expertise within each competency would be required for someone to be successful in those positions?

Start looking for opportunities to develop accomplishments in those areas *now* to prove that you are ready for the higher level positions *later*. By the time you're being considered for the new level, it should be clear to the decision-makers that you've been working at that higher level for some time.

Promote your career by making sure your managers know your competencies.

How many times have you heard other employees complain that they didn't get a particular assignment or position because the manager didn't realize that they'd done similar work in the past? Don't let that happen to you. Try to make sure that your managers know about your competencies and skills that are *not* being used in your current position—but that could be used in the future.

For example, if you've just heard that your company is acquiring a company based in Brazil, and you spent five years living there before college, understand the culture, and are fluent in Portuguese, make sure the right managers know about your background. These skills would be considered as part of competencies such as "Multicultural Sensitivities" or "Interpersonal Understanding." Even if you've told them once about your Brazilian experience, your managers may not remember it now and should be reminded. Even if these are not critical competencies for your position, it is clearly a benefit to the company and could lead to new opportunities, promotions, and growth for you.

Make sure that your manager is aware when you have an accomplishment related to the competencies you're currently being measured against. Simply stop by your manager's office or call them over when they walk by and tell them how excited you are about a particular project going well—and tell them the result (and if they don't know, your role in the project).

Submit an updated list of your latest accomplishments to your manager before each performance appraisal.

You are in charge of your career and advancement. Using your competency-based tracking system will help you make sure your managers have the latest information about your accomplishments and how you are developing your competencies. This will help you professionally to receive a more accurate performance review and to hopefully land that next critical promotion. Who knows—you may be your manager's next choice for a key project that is exciting *and* expands your knowledge and competency base.

When you prepare your updated list of competencies and accomplishments, you should also update your resume to be ready for new opportunities. Consider handing the updated resume to your manager during the performance review if you know you are almost ready for a promotion or a new assignment. (If you do this, please remember to explain to your manager that you've updated your resume for this discussion and to be ready for opportunities within the organization.) It may help remind your manager about competencies that you demonstrated in other assignments—before you were working in your current position.

Hint: Here's one specific suggestion. About one month before your performance appraisal, give your manager a list of the competencies for your position, and provide the manager with accomplishment statements describing what you did in each competency area during the period you are being evaluated. If you've maintained the tracking system for competencies, this should be fairly easy to put together.

Note for Managers

If you are a manager, and you follow these recommendations not only for your own career but for your department, do you see how powerful having the employees more involved with the process would be? Your employees would have a larger stake in improving the competency level of the whole department. And if the competencies in your department are perceived as being at a higher level, that benefits the entire organization.

Note for Human Resources and Training Professionals

Identifying competency gaps and designing training to fill these gaps can be extremely challenging. If you ask each employee to maintain a competency-based tracking system, you would have a stronger understanding of where the gaps are, and be better able to develop training and coaching to help bridge those gaps. Getting more employee participation in the process will help ensure that employees "buy in" to your programs and will improve your own knowledge of where the opportunities might be to improve the overall employee knowledge base.

As new competency needs become evident, you'll be better able to help managers identify the employees available in the organization who have the right competencies for the new initiatives, projects, and programs.

Conclusion

Completing a high-quality competency-based resume is only the first step toward managing your career more effectively at a competency-based organization. But it is an important first step.

You've learned some subtleties about competencies and how to write accomplishment statements that will help you be more successful within your organization. Even though competency-based applications have been used for the last 20 years, more organizations are identifying competencies and adopting this approach every year. In today's working environment, being hard-working, smart, and accomplished isn't enough to ensure success. You also have to be savvy and learn how to make the system within your organization work for you.

In this book, we've given you some hints to get your resume to the top of the pile. Remember that the gold star above the resumes on the cover of this book is only one example of how far you can go if you figure out how to thrive in a competency-based organization. You can see the sky…you *can* get there from here.

**"It's not the will to win,
but the will to prepare to win
that makes the difference."**

—Paul "Bear" Bryant

Key Points for Chapter 14	
"You can't build a reputation on what you are going to do." —Henry Ford	
Key Questions	**Answers**
Now that I am hired, how do I move ahead within the company?	It is critical that you understand the organization's culture and the competencies you'll be measured against as soon as possible after starting your new job.
What are some practical ways to thrive in a competency-based company?	Set up a competency-based tracking system. Include accomplishments related to the competencies identified for your current position and for positions you are interested in for the future.
How do I promote my competencies?	Learning to promote your competencies will make a tremendous difference in your career. Here's how you do it: 1. Set up and use a system to track your competencies and accomplishments. 2. Keep your competency-based resume updated. 3. Develop your critical competencies to a higher level. 4. Identify and overcome your competency gaps. 5. Add new competencies that might be critical in future positions. 6. Promote your career by making sure your managers know your competencies. 7. Submit an updated list of latest accomplishments to your manager before each performance appraisal.

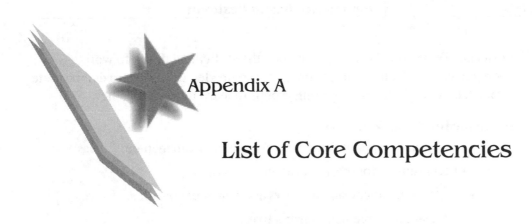

Appendix A

List of Core Competencies

I. Competencies Dealing With People
The Leading Others Cluster

☐ Establishing Focus: The ability to develop and communicate goals in support of the business mission.

- Acts to align own unit's goals with the strategic direction of the business.

- Ensures that people in the unit understand how their work relates to the business mission.

- Ensures that everyone understands and identifies with the unit's mission.

- Ensures that the unit develops goals and a plan to help fulfill the business mission.

☐ Providing Motivational Support: The ability to enhance others' commitment to their work.

- Recognizes and rewards people for their achievements.

- Acknowledges and thanks people for their contributions.

- Expresses pride in the group and encourages people to feel good about their accomplishments.

- Finds creative ways to make people's work rewarding.

- Signals own commitment to a process by being personally present and involved at key events.

- Identifies and promptly tackles morale problems.

- Gives talks or presentations that energize groups.

☐ Fostering Teamwork: As a team member, the ability and desire to work cooperatively with others on a team; as a team leader, the ability to demonstrate interest, skill, and success in getting groups to learn to work together.

Behavior for Team Members

- Listens and responds constructively to other team members' ideas.
- Offers support for others' ideas and proposals.
- Is open with other team members about his/her concerns.
- Expresses disagreement constructively.
- Reinforces team members for their contributions.
- Gives honest and constructive feedback to other team members.
- Provides assistance to others when they need it.
- Works for solutions that all team members can support.
- Shares his/her expertise with others.
- Seeks opportunities to work on teams as a means to develop experience and knowledge.
- Provides assistance, information, or support to others to build or maintain relationships with them.

Behavior for Team Leaders

- Provides opportunities for people to learn to work together as a team.
- Enlists the active participation of everyone.
- Promotes cooperation with other work units.
- Ensures that all team members are treated fairly.
- Recognizes and encourages the behaviors that contribute to teamwork.

☐ Empowering Others: The ability to convey confidence in the ability of employees to be successful, especially at challenging new tasks; delegating significant responsibility and authority; allowing employees freedom to decide how they will accomplish their goals and resolve issues.

- Gives people latitude to make decisions in their own sphere of work.
- Is able to let others make decisions and take charge.
- Encourages individuals and groups to set their own goals, consistent with business goals.
- Expresses confidence in the ability of others to be successful.
- Encourages groups to resolve problems on their own; avoids prescribing a solution.

☐ Managing Change: The ability to demonstrate support for innovation and for organizational changes needed to improve the organization's effectiveness; initiating, sponsoring, and implementing organizational change; helping others to successfully manage organizational change.

Employee Behaviors

- Personally develops a new method or approach.

- Proposes new approaches, methods, or technologies.

- Develops better, faster, or less expensive ways to do things.

Manager/Leader Behaviors

- Works cooperatively with others to produce innovative solutions.

- Takes the lead in setting new business directions, partnerships, policies, or procedures.

- Seizes opportunities to influence the future direction of an organizational unit or the overall business.

- Helps employees to develop a clear understanding of what they will need to do differently, as a result of changes in the organization.

- Implements or supports various change management activities.

- Establishes structures and processes to plan and manage the orderly implementation of change.

- Helps individuals and groups manage the anxiety associated with significant change.

- Facilitates groups or teams through the problem-solving and creative-thinking processes leading to the development and implementation of new approaches, systems, structures, and methods.

☐ Developing Others: The ability to delegate responsibility and to work with others and coach them to develop their capabilities.

- Provides helpful, behaviorally specific feedback to others.

- Shares information, advice, and suggestions to help others be more successful; provides effective coaching.

- Gives people assignments that will help develop their abilities.

- Regularly meets with employees to review their developmental progress.

- Recognizes and reinforces people's developmental efforts and improvements.

- Expresses confidence in the ability of others to be successful.

☐ Managing Performance: The ability to take responsibility for one's own, or one's employees' performance, by setting clear goals and expectations, tracking progress against the goals, ensuring feedback, and addressing performance problems and issues promptly.

Employee Behaviors

- With his manager, sets specific, measurable goals that are realistic but challenging, with dates for accomplishment.

- With his manager, clarifies expectations about what will be done and how.

- Enlists his manager's support in obtaining the information, resources, and training needed to accomplish his work effectively.

- Promptly notifies his manager about any problems that affect his ability to accomplish planned goals.

- Seeks performance feedback from his manager and from others with whom he interacts on the job.

- Prepares a personal development plan with specific goals and a timeline for their accomplishment.

- Takes significant action to develop skills needed for effectiveness in current or future job.

Manager/Leader Behaviors

- Ensures that employees have clear goals and responsibilities.

- Works with employees to set and communicate performance standards that are specific and measurable.

- Supports employees in their efforts to achieve job goals.

- Stays informed about employees' progress and performance through both formal and informal methods.

- Provides specific performance feedback, both positive and corrective, as soon as possible after an event.

- Deals firmly and promptly with performance problems; lets people know what is expected of them and when.

Communication and Influencing Cluster

☐ Attention to Communication: The ability to ensure that information is passed on to others who should be kept informed.

- Ensures that others involved in a project or effort are kept informed about developments and plans.

- Ensures that important information from his management is shared with his employees and others as appropriate.

- Shares ideas and information with others who might find them useful.

- Uses multiple channels or means to communicate important messages.

- Keeps his manager informed about progress and problems; avoids surprises.

- Ensures that regular, consistent communication takes place.

☐ Oral Communication: The ability to express oneself clearly in conversations and interactions with others.

- Speaks clearly and can be easily understood.

- Tailors the content of speech to the level and experience of the audience.

- Uses appropriate grammar and choice of words in oral speech.

- Organizes ideas clearly in oral speech.

- Expresses ideas concisely in oral speech.

- Maintains eye contact when speaking with others.

- Summarizes or paraphrases his understanding of what others have said to verify understanding and prevent miscommunication.

☐ Written Communication: The ability to express oneself clearly in business writing.

- Expresses ideas clearly and concisely in writing.

- Organizes written ideas clearly and signals the organization to the reader.

- Tailors written communications to effectively reach an audience.

- Uses graphics and other aids to clarify complex or technical information.

- Spells correctly.

- Writes using concrete, specific language.

- Uses punctuation correctly.

- Writes grammatically.

- Uses an appropriate business writing style.

☐ Persuasive Communication: The ability to plan and deliver oral and written communications that make an impact and persuade their intended audiences.

- Identifies and presents information or data that will have a strong effect on others.

- Selects language and examples tailored to the level and experience of the audience.

- Selects stories, analogies, or examples to illustrate a point.

- Creates graphics, overheads, or slides that display information clearly and with high impact.

- Presents several different arguments in support of a position.

☐ Interpersonal Awareness: The ability to notice, interpret, and anticipate others' concerns and feelings, and to communicate this awareness empathetically to others.

- Understands the interests and important concerns of others.

- Notices and accurately interprets what others are feeling, based on their choice of words, tone of voice, expressions, and other nonverbal behavior.

- Anticipates how others will react to a situation.

- Listens attentively to people's ideas and concerns.

- Understands both the strengths and the weaknesses of others.

- Understands the unspoken meaning in a situation.

- Says or does things to address others' concerns.

- Finds nonthreatening ways to approach others about sensitive issues.

- Makes others feel comfortable by responding in ways that convey interest in what they have to say.

☐ Influencing Others: The ability to gain others' support for ideas, proposals, projects, and solutions.

- Presents arguments that address others' most important concerns and issues and looks for win-win solutions.

- Involves others in a process or decision to ensure their support.

- Offers trade-offs or exchanges to gain commitment.

- Identifies and proposes solutions that benefit all parties involved in a situation.

- Enlists expert or third parties to influence others.

- Develops other indirect strategies to influence others.

- Knows when to escalate critical issues to management, if own efforts to enlist support have not succeeded.

- Structures situations to create a desired impact and to maximize the chances of a favorable outcome.

- Works to make a particular impression on others.

- Identifies and targets influence efforts at the real decision-makers and those who can influence them.

- Seeks out and builds relationships with others who can provide information, intelligence, career support, potential business, and other forms of help.

- Takes a personal interest in others to develop relationships.

- Accurately anticipates the implications of events or decisions for various stakeholders in the organization, and plans strategy accordingly.

☐ Building Collaborative Relationships: The ability to develop, maintain, and strengthen partnerships with others inside or outside the organization who can provide information, assistance, and support.

- Asks about the other person's personal experiences, interests, and family.

- Asks questions to identify shared interests, experiences, or other common ground.

- Shows an interest in what others have to say; acknowledges their perspectives and ideas.

- Recognizes the business concerns and perspectives of others.

- Expresses gratitude and appreciation to others who have provided information, assistance, or support.

- Takes time to get to know coworkers, to build rapport and establish a common bond.

- Tries to build relationships with people whose assistance, cooperation, and support may be needed.

- Provides assistance, information, and support to others to build a basis for future reciprocity.

☐ Customer Orientation: The ability to demonstrate concern for satisfying one's external and/or internal customers.

- Quickly and effectively solves customer problems.

- Talks to customers to find out what they want and how satisfied they are with what they are getting.

- Lets customers know he is willing to work with them to meet their needs.

- Finds ways to measure and track customer satisfaction.

- Presents a cheerful, positive manner with customers.

II. Competencies Dealing With Business
The Preventing and Solving Problems Cluster

☐ Diagnostic Information Gathering: The ability to identify the information needed to clarify a situation, seek that information from appropriate sources, and use skillful questioning to draw out the information, when others are reluctant to disclose it.

- Identifies the specific information needed to clarify a situation or to make a decision.

- Gets more complete and accurate information by checking multiple sources.

- Probes skillfully to get at the facts, when others are reluctant to provide full, detailed information.

- Routinely walks around to see how people are doing and to hear about any problems they are encountering.

- Questions others to assess whether they have thought through a plan of action.

- Questions others to assess their confidence in solving a problem or tackling a situation.

- Asks questions to clarify a situation.

- Seeks the perspective of everyone involved in a situation.

- Seeks out knowledgeable people to obtain information or clarify a problem.

☐ Analytical Thinking: The ability to tackle a problem by using a logical, systematic, sequential approach.

- Makes a systematic comparison of two or more alternatives.

- Notices discrepancies and inconsistencies in available information.

- Identifies a set of features, parameters, or considerations to take into account in analyzing a situation or making a decision.

- Approaches a complex task or problem by breaking it down into its component parts and considering each part in detail.

- Weighs the costs, benefits, risks, and chances for success in making a decision.

- Identifies many possible causes for a problem.

- Carefully weighs the priority of things to be done.

☐ Forward Thinking: The ability to anticipate the implications and consequences of situations and take appropriate action to be prepared for possible contingencies.

- Anticipates possible problems and develops contingency plans in advance.
- Notices trends in the industry or marketplace and develops plans to prepare for opportunities or problems.
- Anticipates the consequences of situations and plans accordingly.
- Anticipates how individuals and groups will react to situations and information and plans accordingly.

☐ Conceptual Thinking: The ability to find effective solutions by taking a holistic, abstract, or theoretical perspective.

- Notices similarities between different and apparently unrelated situations.
- Quickly identifies the central or underlying issues in a complex situation.
- Creates a graphic diagram showing a systems view of the situation.
- Develops analogies or metaphors to explain a situation.
- Applies a theoretical framework to understand a specific situation.

☐ Strategic Thinking: The ability to analyze the organization's competitive position by considering market and industry trends, existing and potential customers, and strengths and weaknesses as compared to competitors.

- Understands the organization's strengths and weaknesses as compared to competitors.
- Understands industry and market trends affecting the organization's competitiveness.
- Has an in-depth understanding of competitive products and services within the marketplace.
- Develops and proposes a long-term strategy for the organization based on an analysis of the industry and marketplace and the organization's current and potential capabilities as compared to competitors.

☐ Technical Expertise: The ability to demonstrate depth of knowledge and skill in a technical area.

- Effectively applies technical knowledge to solve a range of problems.
- Possesses an in-depth knowledge and skill in a technical area.
- Develops technical solutions to new or highly complex problems that cannot be solved using existing methods or approaches.
- Is sought out as an expert to provide advice or solutions in his technical area.
- Keeps informed about cutting-edge technology in his technical area.

The Achieving Results Cluster

☐ Initiative: Identifying what needs to be done and doing it before being asked or before the situation requires it.

- Identifying what needs to be done and taking action before being asked or the situation requires it.

- Does more than what is normally required in a situation.

- Seeks out others involved in a situation to learn their perspectives.

- Takes independent action to change the direction of events.

☐ Entrepreneurial Orientation: The ability to look for and seize profitable business opportunities; willingness to take calculated risks to achieve business goals.

- Notices and seizes profitable business opportunities.

- Stays abreast of business, industry, and market information that may reveal business opportunities.

- Demonstrates willingness to take calculated risks to achieve business goals.

- Proposes innovative business deals to potential customers, suppliers, and business partners.

- Encourages and supports entrepreneurial behavior in others.

☐ Fostering Innovation: The ability to develop, sponsor, or support the introduction of new and improved methods, products, procedures, or technologies.

- Personally develops a new product or service.

- Personally develops a new method or approach.

- Sponsors the development of new products, services, methods, or procedures.

- Proposes new approaches, methods, or technologies.

- Develops better, faster, or less expensive ways to do things.

- Works cooperatively with others to produce innovative solutions.

☐ Results Orientation: The ability to focus on the desired result of one's own or one's unit's work, setting challenging goals. Focusing effort on the goals, and meeting or exceeding them.

- Develops challenging but achievable goals.

- Develops clear goals for meetings and projects.

- Maintains commitment to goals in the face of obstacles and frustration.

- Finds or creates ways to measure performance against goals.

- Exerts unusual effort over time to achieve a goal.

- Has a strong sense of urgency about solving problems and getting work done.

☐ Thoroughness: Ensuring that one's own work and information are complete and accurate; carefully preparing for meetings and presentations; following up with others to ensure that agreements and commitments have been fulfilled.

- Sets up procedures to ensure high quality of work.

- Monitors the quality of work.

- Verifies information.

- Checks the accuracy of own and other's work.

- Develops and uses systems to organize and keep track of information or work progress.

- Carefully prepares for meetings and presentations.

- Organizes information or material for others.

- Carefully reviews and checks the accuracy of information in work reports provided by management, IT, or other individuals and groups.

☐ Decisiveness: The ability to make decisions in a timely manner.

- Is willing to make decisions in difficult or ambiguous situations, when time is critical.

- Takes charge of a group when it is necessary to facilitate change, overcome an impasse, face issues, or ensure decisions are made.

- Makes tough decisions.

III. Self-Management Competencies

☐ Self-Confidence: Faith in one's own ideas and capability to be successful; willingness to take an independent position in the face of opposition.

- Is confident of own ability to accomplish goals.

- Presents self crisply and impressively.

- Is willing to speak up to the right person or group at the right time, when he disagrees with a decision or strategy.

- Approaches challenging tasks with a "can-do" attitude.

☐ Stress Management: The ability to keep functioning effectively when under pressure and maintain self-control in the face of hostility or provocation.

- Remains calm under stress.

- Can effectively handle several problems or tasks at once.

- Controls his response when criticized, attacked, or provoked.

- Maintains a sense of humor under difficult circumstances.

- Manages own behavior to prevent or reduce feelings of stress.

☐ Personal Credibility: Demonstrated concern that one be perceived as responsible, reliable, and trustworthy.

- Does what he commits to doing.

- Respects the confidentiality of information or concerns shared by others.

- Is honest and forthright with people.

- Carries his fair share of the workload.

- Takes responsibility for own mistakes; does not blame others.

- Conveys a command of the relevant facts and information.

☐ Flexibility: Openness to different and new ways of doing things; willingness to modify one's preferred way of doing things.

- Is able to see the merits of perspectives other than his own.

- Demonstrates openness to new organizational structures, procedures, and technology.

- Switches to a different strategy when an initially selected one is unsuccessful.

- Demonstrates willingness to modify a strongly held position in the face of contrary evidence.

(From *The Value-Added Employee* by Edward J. Cripe and Richard S. Mansfield. Copyright © 2002 by Butterworth-Heinemann. Reprinted with permission of Elsevier Ltd.)

Appendix B

Typical Competencies for Certain Professions

Technical Professionals	
Achievement Orientation • Measures performance. • Improves outcomes. • Sets challenging goals. • Innovates. **Impact and Influence** • Uses direct persuasion, and facts and figures. • Gives presentations tailored to the audience. • Shows concern with professional reputation. **Conceptual Thinking** • Recognizes key actions and underlying problems. • Makes connections and identifies patterns. **Analytical Thinking** • Anticipates obstacles. • Breaks problems apart systematically. • Makes logical conclusions. • Sees consequences and implications. **Initiative** • Persists in problem-solving. • Addresses problems before being asked to.	**Self-Confidence** • Expresses confidence in own judgment. • Seeks challenges and independence. **Interpersonal Understanding** • Understands attitudes, interests, and needs of others. **Concern for Order** • Seeks clarity of roles and information. • Checks quality of work or information. • Keeps records. **Information Seeking** • Contacts many different sources. • Reads industry publications to stay current. **Teamwork and Cooperation** • Brainstorms and asks for input. • Credits others. **Expertise** • Expands and uses technical knowledge. • Enjoys technical work and shares expertise. **Customer Service Orientation** • Discovers and meets underlying needs of internal and external customers.

Managers

Impact and Influence
- Concern with personal impact.
- Calculating effect of words or actions on others.
- Effective with direct persuasion.
- Adapts presentation to specific audiences.
- Uses experts or other third parties.
- Makes others feel ownership of own solutions.

Achievement Orientation
- Measures results, and thinks and talks about measurements.
- Finds better, more efficient, and faster ways of doing things.
- Sets specific, challenging goals.
- Makes cost-benefit analysis.
- Takes calculated entrepreneurial risks.
- Concern for innovation.
- Makes good job-person matches to improve performance.

Teamwork and Cooperation
- Solicit input of others and involve others in issues that may affect them.
- Gives credit and recognition.
- Encourages and empowers group.
- Works to improve group morale; to develop teamwork and cooperation.
- Resolves conflicts.

Analytical Thinking
- Sees implications or consequences.
- Analyzes situations systematically to determine cause or consequences.
- Anticipates obstacles and plans way to deal with them.
- Thinks ahead about steps in process.
- Analyzes what is needed to accomplish goal.

Initiative
- Seizes opportunities as they arise.
- Handles crises swiftly and effectively.
- Tenacity and persistence in reaching goal.
- Willingness to work long hours as needed.

Developing Others
- Giving constructive feedback.
- Providing reassurance and encouragement after difficulties.
- Coaching.
- Giving specific developmental assignments or training.

Self-Confidence
- Confidence in own ability and judgment.
- Enjoys challenging tasks.
- Directly questions and challenges actions of superiors.
- Takes personal responsibility for problems.

Interpersonal Understanding
- Understands attitudes, interests, needs, and perspectives of others.
- Interprets nonverbal behavior; understands moods and feelings.
- Knowing what motivates others.
- Understanding strengths and limitations of others.
- Understanding reasons for others' behavior.

Directiveness/Assertiveness
- Sets limits.
- Says no when necessary.
- Sets standards and demands performance.
- Confronts performance problems.

Information Seeking
- Systematic information gathering.
- Seeking information from many sources.
- Getting out to see or touch the situation.

Team Leadership
- Setting and communicating high standards for group performance.
- Standing up for the group in relation to the larger organization.
- Obtaining needed resources for the group.

Conceptual Thinking
- Seeing connections or patterns not obvious to others.
- Noticing inconsistencies or discrepancies.
- Rapidly identifying key issues/actions in complex situations.
- Using vigorous, original analogies or metaphors.

Organizational Awareness and Relationship Building

Expertise/Specialized Knowledge
- Judging what is a challenging but achievable goal and what is a moderate risk.

Salespeople

Impact and Influence
- Establishes credibility.
- Addresses customer's issues and concerns
- Indirect influence.
- Predicts effect of own words and actions.

Achievement Orientation
- Sets challenging, achievable goals.
- Uses time efficiently.
- Improves customer's operations.
- Focuses on potential profit opportunities.

Initiative
- Persists—does not give up easily.
- Seizes opportunities.
- Responds to competitive threats.

Interpersonal Understanding
- Understands nonverbal behavior.
- Understands others' attitudes and meanings.
- Predicts others' reactions.

Customer Service Orientation
- Makes extra effort to meet customer needs.
- Discovers and meets customer's underlying needs.
- Follows up on customer contacts and complaints.
- Becomes a trusted adviser to customers.

Self-Confidence
- Confident in own abilities.
- Takes on challenges.
- Optimistic style.

Relationship Building
- Maintains work-related friendships.
- Has and uses network of contacts.

Analytical Thinking
- Anticipates and prepares for obstacles.
- Thinks of several explanations or plans.

Conceptual Thinking
- Uses rules of thumb.
- Notices similarities between past and present.

Information Seeking
- Gets information from many sources.

Organizational Awareness
- Understands functioning of client organization.

Technical Expertise
- Has relevant technical or product knowledge.

College Professors/Teachers

Student-Centered Orientation
- Has positive expectations of students.
- Attends to students concerns.

Humanistic Learning Orientation
- Values the learning process.
- Views specialized knowledge as a resource.

Creating a Context Conducive to Adult Learning
- Works to understand student frame of reference.
- Works to establish mutuality and rapport.
- Holds students accountable to their best learning interests.

Grounding Learning Objectives in an Analysis of Students' Needs
- Actively seeks information about students.
- Diagnoses.
- Prescribes action.

Facilitating the Learning Process
- Links pedagogy to students' concerns.
- Structures processes to facilitate students' active learning.
- Adapts to situational demands.
- Responds to nonverbal cues.

Helping and Human Services Professionals
(nurses, physicians, teachers, professors, organizational-effectiveness consultants, and alcoholism counselors)

Impact and Influence
- Establishes credibility.
- Tailors presentation and language for audience.
- Individual influence strategies.
- Uses examples, humor, body language, voice.

Developing Others
- Innovative teaching methods.
- Flexible response to individual needs.
- Belief in students' potential.

Interpersonal Understanding
- Takes time to listen to others' problems.
- Is aware of others' moods and feelings.
- Understands body language.
- Aware of others' background, interests, and needs.
- May understand long-term situations in depth.

Self-Confidence
- Confident in own abilities and judgment.
- Takes responsibilities for problems and failings.
- Questions and gives suggestions to superiors.

Self-Control
- Keeps own emotions from interfering with work.
- Avoids inappropriate involvement with clients, etc.
- Stress-resistant—has stamina, humor.

Other Personal Effectiveness Competencies
- Accurate self-assessment—learns from mistakes.
- Finds work in occupation enjoyable.
- Organizational commitment—aligns self with mission.
- Genuinely likes people.
- Positive expectations of others.

Professional Expertise
- Expands and uses professional knowledge.

Customer Service Orientation
- Discovers and works to meet underlying needs.
- Follows through on questions, requests and complaints.

Teamwork and Cooperation
- Solicits input.
- Credits and cooperates with others.

Analytical Thinking
- Sees causal relationships and makes inferences.
- Systematically breaks apart complex problems.

Conceptual Thinking
- Recognizes patterns.
- Uses concepts to diagnose situations.
- Makes connections; develops theories.
- Simplifies/clarifies difficult material.

Initiative
- Does more than is required in job.
- Responds quickly/decisively in a crisis.

Flexibility
- Adapts style and tactics to fit circumstances.

Directiveness/Assertiveness
- Sets limits and says no when necessary.
- Confronts problem behavior.

Appendix C

Competencies That Will Be Important in the Future

Executives	Strategic Thinking	Ability to understand rapidly changing environmental trends, market opportunities, competitive threats, organization strengths/weaknesses to identify best strategic response.
	Change Leadership	Ability to communicate a compelling vision of the organization's strategy that makes adapting to change appear possible and desirable.
	Relationship Management	Ability to establish relationships (with no direct authority) and influence others whose cooperation is needed.
Managers	Flexibility	Willingness and ability to change managerial structures and processes when needed to implement organization's change strategies.
	Change Implementation	Ability to communicate organization's needs for change to coworkers and in the department or workgroup.
	Entrepreneurial Innovation	Motivation to champion new products, services, and processes.
	Interpersonal Understanding	Ability to understand and value ideas of diverse people.
	Empowering	Using managerial behaviors to make employees feel more capable and motivated to assume greater responsibility.
	Team Facilitation	Group process skills used to get diverse groups of people to work together effectively.
	Intercultural Adaptability	Ability to adapt rapidly to and function effectively in any foreign environment.

Employees	Flexibility	Ability to see change as an opportunity rather than as a threat.
	Information-Seeking Motivation/Ability to Learn	Enthusiasm for opportunities to learn new technical and interpersonal skills.
	Achievement Motivation	Desire to achieve, innovate, and continuously improve quality and productivity to improve competitiveness.
	Work Motivation Under Time Pressure	Ability to work under increasing demands for products and services in less time.
	Collaboration	Ability to work cooperatively in multidisciplinary groups with diverse coworkers.
	Customer Service Orientation	Genuine desire to be of help to others; ability to understand customer needs and overcome obstacles to resolve customer problems.

(From *Competence at Work: Models for Superior Performance* by Lyle M. Spencer, Jr., Ph.D., and Signe M. Spencer. Copyright © 1993 by John Wiley & Sons, Inc. Reprinted with permission of John Wiley & Sons, Inc.)

Appendix D

Quick Reference Competency-Based Cold Call Cover Letters

A competency-based cold call letter can be written when you are interested in working for a particular organization, and there is no position posted (or simply you haven't been able to find out about any open positions). **Your challenge, in your letter, is to create a need for a position.** If you are going to send this kind of letter to an organization, it is important to remember to write it by focusing on the needs—competencies—of the organization. Here are some questions to ask yourself while you are doing your research:

★ XYZ is opening a new division/plant in my area.

    ☆ Will they need professionals in my functional area?

    ☆ What competencies will those people need to demonstrate to be hired?

    ☆ How strong am I in the competencies the new division will need?

★ How can my competencies help an organization that is having problems?

★ I have a great idea for a new product/service. How can I market my idea and my expertise to target organizations?

Once you finish your research and have determined how you can help the organization, you are ready to get started writing a **Competency-Based Cold Call Cover Letter**.

Steps	Action	✓
1. Research the competencies the organization may need for the relevant positions in your professional area.	Make a list of competencies to address in your resume and your cover letter.	
2. Find a specific name to address your letter to.	Write your letter using the name of the person who can make a decision to hire you, if at all possible. Immediate supervisors and managers are best if you can find them on the organization's Website, on Hoover's, or in an association directory. If you don't find them, you can always try to call the company and ask. Make sure you get the right spelling for the contact's name.	
3. Write your first paragraph.	Your opening paragraph should be dynamic, create a need, and tell them why you are writing. What is the position you believe they might need filled? • Be energetic (use action verbs) and positive. • Use competency language or synonyms. • Tell them how you will help the organization succeed.	
4. Write the middle paragraph(s).	• Give some examples to demonstrate how strong you are in key competency areas that would help their organization. • Use different examples/accomplishments than the ones in your resume. • Tell them how you will help them (reduce costs, make money, save time, etc.) by emphasizing how your competencies, strengths, and skills are valuable to help them with their organization's problems or to capitalize on opportunities.	
5. Write the closing paragraph.	1. Tell them what you want from them. It could be: • An interview. • A meeting to discuss their needs. • The name of their recruiter. 2. Don't forget to tell them you will call as a follow-up in the near future (or in a week). 3. Refer them to your enclosed resume.	

Appendix E

How to Write Competency-Based Thank You Letters

Getting Ready to Write Your Letter

During the interview, remember to always get business cards from the people who interviewed you.

Thank you notes can be sent using e-mail, note cards, or as a formal letter.

1. *Immediately* after your interview, take some notes.
   Ask yourself these questions:
   a. What *competencies* did I learn the organization needs (for the position I'm interviewing for)?
   b. Was there a *competency* they mentioned that I didn't talk about in the interview, emphasize enough, or include in my resume?
   c. What did each interviewer discuss that I was impressed with?
   d. Was there something I could have explained better? Was there something I wanted to say that I missed?
   e. What more did I learn about the company in the interview?
   f. What did I learn about the corporate culture and management style?
   g. How did I feel about the interview?

2. When addressing your thank you letter, use the business cards you collected.
   a. Make sure all names and titles are spelled correctly.
   b. Address each thank you letter to a specific person.

Writing Your Competency-Based Thank You Letter

1. First, state that you enjoyed the interview, and thank the interviewer.
2. Second, tell them something *new* about how you are even more convinced you can meet their needs.

a. Identify how your *competencies* will benefit the organization (or department).

b. Remember to explain how you can help their organization be more successful (that is, how you will make them money or save them time). **Address their needs from *their* perspective instead of yours.**

c. Relate your comments to something that was said in the interview. (Example: *I was particularly impressed when you talked about....*)

3. Third, tell them that you are interested in the position and would be happy to answer any additional questions. Include a telephone number to make it easier for them to call you.

4. Include a signature line.
   a. Close with "Sincerely,". (Always capitalize, and use a comma after your close.)

5. Do the final edit. Make sure you:
   a. Double-check the accuracy of names and titles.
   b. Use their terminology (or synonyms) in your letter.
   c. Check for grammar, punctuation, and redundancy.
   d. Send your e-mails the day after the interview. Avoid sending them from midnight to 6 a.m.
   e. Mail regular thank you notes or letters within two days of the interview.

Additional hints:
   a. Use e-mail—unless there is a good reason not to.
   b. Use quality, blank note cards if you need to send a handwritten note. Avoid using cards that have "Thank You" written on them. Write legibly.
   c. If you have a business card, you *may* want to enclose that with the note as another way to make it easy to contact you. This will work better with some employers than others, so consider who you are sending it to. This tends to work better with less formal employers. Use your judgment.
   d. If you are sending an electronic thank you note, make sure you follow the same rules as if you were writing a formal letter. Follow all the correct grammar, punctuation and formatting rules.

Thank you notes can give you an edge over other applicants—particularly when they are well written.

Appendix F

The Benefits of Using Competency-Based Filing Systems

It all starts with your competency-based resume!

Organizations that use competency-based applications would strengthen the effectiveness of their programs if they encouraged employees to develop a competency-based "filing system" or "bank." By having employees participate more actively in the process by creating and updating their lists of competencies with accomplishments, organizations will empower their employees and increase the chance employees will be more motivated to succeed.

Setting up the competency-based "filing system" or "bank"	When candidates are hired, a personal competency-based bank or filing system should be created online using a database or spreadsheet program. The competencies the new employees have when they arrive, and the competencies they acquire while employed should be updated, at least monthly, in this bank. Employees will write accomplishment statements and identify the competencies demonstrated for each accomplishment.
Developing and tracking knowledge capital	Organizations using competency-tracking banks can easily determine who has strengths in a particular competency—and where the organization as a whole has strengths and development opportunities. When projects need to be assigned, managers know who has the right competencies to be successful.

Analyzing employee training needs	By using competency-based filing systems, it will be easier to analyze training and development needs to make the organization more effective. Competency gaps are easier to identify and work on closing through training, coaching, and mentoring programs. Where the organization needs stronger competencies, the decision can be made to offer classroom, Internet-based or on-the-job training. Training professionals can use the information to help them target developing key competencies in the training programs they design. Not only does the company have a more competent employee group, the employees are given the opportunity to have more impact on developing their own knowledge, skills, and abilities within the organization.
Conducting performance appraisals	By looking at the information in the competency-based filing system or bank for each employee, managers can give them more accurate performance appraisals—which considers the information employees provided themselves. *Note: some employees may not have the communication skills or self-confidence to promote their competencies and accomplishments effectively. They may need some training or coaching to provide the high quality information an effective competency-based filing system or bank needs to support the potential benefits.*
Planning	Organizations can plan for future projects and make key assignments for the projects more effectively by using the competency-based filing system or bank. Managers can help employees focus and manage performance expectations based on the information in the individual's competency bank
Developing careers	By being able to review, update, and change the information in the competency-based filing system or bank, employees can take a more active role in planning their own career advancement.

Mentoring and coaching	By knowing which competencies each employee has, matching employees with mentors and coaches can be more systematic and productive.
Strategic decision making	When organizations know the competencies of their employees, they are better prepared to sell their strengths, target potential customers and partners, and secure new projects.
Planning employment needs	When future projects are planned, organizations can better project their human capital needs. Competency gaps can be filled by hiring employees with those competencies or developing current employees through training, mentoring, or coaching.
Succession planning	Having an updated, high-quality competency-based filing system or bank can help managers be more aware of the competencies needed to be successful in higher level positions and make better decisions about who has the competencies required for the job.

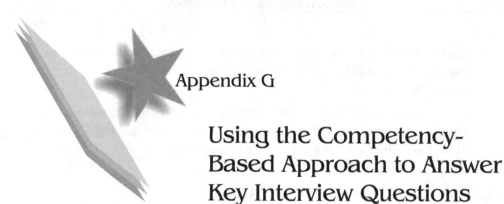

Appendix G

Using the Competency-Based Approach to Answer Key Interview Questions

This appendix gives basic tips on how to answer some of the most common interview questions in a better, more effective way that emphasizes your competencies.

Why Are You Interested in This Position?

Once you've identified the critical competencies the organization is looking for, you need to think about how your own competencies, strengths, and interests match the organization's needs.

Answer questions by focusing on *matching* interests related to the critical competencies based on your experience. The following is an example of how to answer the question, "Why are you interested in this position?" "Three main reasons: it will give me the opportunity to prove that I'm very good at achieving goals, developing productive long-term relationships with customers, and identifying ways to encourage the employees in the department to be even more successful."

Paraphrase the competencies—explain them in your own words. Be prepared to give examples of when you have done these things in the past. Treat even this type of question like a behavioral question, and remember that past behavior is the best predictor of future behavior.

What Are Your Strengths?

Think about the key competencies for the position. What are the competencies the hiring manager needs for his or her department to be as successful as possible? Leave out other strengths that are not as closely related to what the organization needs to be successful. For example, if you are creative and write poetry, you need to remember that this kind of creativity will not be perceived as an asset for a position in finance, accounting, or engineering.

Choose three or four of the competencies that are also your personal strengths, and answer the question about your strengths with these competencies.

⋆ Start with the one that is the most important to the hiring manager's success, and work through the list until you come to the one that is least critical for success.

⋆ Paraphrase. Use synonyms to describe the competencies. It is almost always safer, and you will be perceived as more sophisticated if you avoid using the exact words from the competency list.

What Is Your Biggest Weakness?

Most career consultants will tell candidates that they should pick a weakness and turn it into a strength with their answer to this question. While we agree, in general, with this position, we have a few suggestions that will help you give a better answer to this question. You want your answer to be diplomatically honest and for it to be perceived as original and real by the interviewer. Stay away from cookie-cutter answers to this question. Remember that everyone has weaknesses, so saying you have no weaknesses is not believable.

First, remember to stay away from any answer directly related to the key competencies for the position. You do not want to be perceived as weak at "Impact and Influence" if that is key to being successful in the position.

Second, try to pick something that the interviewer may have noticed as a weakness already in the interview. Here's an example that fits a number of people: "I'm not always as concise as I think I should be. It's something I'm aware of, and I'm working on it, but I know I could improve." This answer could be tailored to fit someone who will go off on a tangent during the interview without much effort.

Another approach is to focus on something different that might be a little humorous. One of our clients was originally from West Virginia and was getting ready for an interview in Texas. We coached him to answer this way: "I don't know if you've noticed, but some people down here think I have a little bit of an accent. It causes them to underestimate me. While they are doing this, they tell me all sorts of information before they finally figure out I know what I am doing. But it can also work against me." Do you see why this answer worked well for the client?

Tell Me About Yourself

Throughout this book, we've emphasized the need to think about the employer's needs first and your own *fit* second. So the key question here is: 'What about you does the employer need to know to realize you have the competencies he or she needs to help their organization be more successful?

Limit your answer to no more than two minutes. Focus on your work experience. Human resources professionals tell horror stories about people volunteering that they've been divorced four times, have a terminal illness, help proselytize for their church, or that their three children can be a real handful in the interview. You are a professional; your answer to this question needs to stay professional and away from emphasizing your private, personal life.

There are two typical approaches to answering this question. The traditional answer is primarily chronological—start from the beginning and work your way to more current information. The second approach is to briefly touch on your early background and education, but spend more of your two minutes focused on your current strengths, skills, and abilities and what you want to do next.

Both approaches can work well for people, but one may be more effective for you, depending on your own situation. Be logical, organized, and concise. The interviewer may also be evaluating your skills as a communicator or presenter while listening to the content.

Remember that both approaches can be stronger if the individual keeps in mind that one of their goals is to demonstrate in their answer to this question that they are strong in the competency areas the organization has identified for the position they are interviewing for.

Chapter Notes

Chapter 2

[1] Conversation with Signe Spencer, April 14, 2004.

[2] 2002 Recruitment and Retention Survey conducted by the Chartered Institute of Personnel and Development (the professional association for personnel and HR specialists in the United Kingdom and the Republic of Ireland).

[3] Spencer conversation.

[4] Lyle M. Spencer and Signe Spencer, *Competence at Work: Models for Superior Performance* (New York: John Wiley & Sons, 1993), 9.

[5] Adapted from Robert Wood and Tim Payne. *Competency-Based Recruitment and Selection: A Practical Guide* (Chichester, England: John Wiley & Sons, 1998), 28.

Chapter 3

[1] Adapted from *Competency-Based Recruitment and Selection*, 27.

[2] Spencer conversation.

[3] Neil Rankin, "Competency & Emotional Intelligence Benchmarking, 2003/04," IRS 2003.

[4] Spencer conversation.

Chapter 5

[1] Ron Fry, *101 Great Resumes: Winning Resumes for Any Situation, Any Job, Any Career* (Franklin Lakes, N.J.: Career Press, 2002), 40.

Bibliography

Boyatzis, Richard. *The Competent Manager: A Model for Effective Performance*. New York: John Wiley & Sons, Inc., 1982.

Cooper, Kenneth Carlton. *Effective Competency Modeling and Reporting: A Step-by-Step Guide for Improving Individual & Organizational Performance*. New York: Amacom, 2000.

Cripe, Edward J., and Richard S. Mansfield. *The Value-Added Employee: 31 Competencies to Make Yourself Irresistible to Any Company*. Wodburn, Mass.: Butterworth-Heinemann, 2002.

Fein, Richard. *Cover Letters! Cover Letters! Cover Letters!* Franklin Lakes, N.J.: Career Press, 1996.

Fry, Ron. *101 Great Resumes*. Franklin Lakes, N.J.: Career Press, 2002.

Green, Paul C. *Building Robust Competencies: Linking Human Resources Systems to Organizational Strategies*. San Francisco: Jossey-Bass, 1999.

Smith, Rebecca. *Electronic Resumes and Online Networking, 2nd Edition*. Franklin Lakes, N.J.: Career Press, 2000.

Spencer, Lyle M., Jr., Ph.D., and Signe M. Spencer. *Competence at Work: Models for Superior Performance*. New York: John Wiley & Sons, Inc., 1993.

Toropov, Brandon. *Last Minute Cover Letters*. Franklin Lakes, N.J.: Career Press, 1996.

United States Office of Personnel Management, "Mosaic Competencies: Leadership Effectiveness Study, 1992," http://www.opm.gov/deu/Handbook_2003/DEOH-MOSAIC-4.asp.

Wendleton, Kate. *Interviewing and Salary Negotiation*. Franklin Lakes, N.J.: Career Press, 1999.

Wood, Robert, and Tim Payne. *Competency-Based Recruitment and Selection: A Practical Guide*. Chichester, England: John Wiley & Sons, 1998.

Bibliography

Index

About the Authors

ROBIN KESSLER is president of The Interview Coach, a human resources and career consulting firm based in Houston; she also teaches Interviewing Skills and Business and Professional Communication as an adjunct professor for University of Houston-Downtown. Robin has more than 20 years of experience improving resumes, interviews, presentations, and organization communication as a human resources professional, consultant, and career coach. She has written articles on current issues in speaking skills and organization communication for publications including *HR Magazine* and the *Houston Chronicle*, and has been a guest speaker at conferences and on radio and television programs. Robin received her B.A. and M.B.A. from Northwestern University. Please contact her with your comments at robin@competencybasedcareers.com or 713.831.6881.

LINDA A. STRASBURG is a business owner and consultant based in Salt Lake City who specializes in training and career coaching; her company is LightsOn-Network. She presents seminars, speaks, and writes on a broad spectrum of business and human resource topics. Linda also teaches college students and coaches employees to develop their career, job-search and personal-development skills. She was a Director of Education for a local college, and Director of Development for an e-learning company. For the last 11 years she has hosted a radio talk show *InterViews & InterActions* that broadcasts in Salt Lake City, and worldwide on the Internet. She has interviewed hundreds of guests on the cutting-edge of business and personal development. Linda has a master's degree in professional communication (MPC) and holds an undergraduate degree in human resource management. She can be reached via e-mail at LightsOnNetwork@comcast.net. Her Website is *www.LightsOn-Network.com*.